# JIM BEAM
# BOURBON COOKBOOK

# JIM BEAM

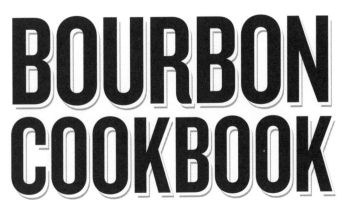

# BOURBON COOKBOOK

### OVER 70 RECIPES & COCKTAILS TO MAKE WITH BOURBON

*James B. Beam*
NONE GENUINE WITHOUT MY SIGNATURE

**Thunder Bay Press**
An imprint of Printers Row Publishing Group
10350 Barnes Canyon Road, Suite 100, San Diego, CA 92121
www.thunderbaybooks.com

All notations of errors or omissions should be addressed to Thunder Bay Press, Editorial
Department, at the above address. All other correspondence (author inquiries, permissions)
concerning the content of this book should be addressed to Octopus Publishing Group
Limited, Carmelite House, 50 Victoria Embankment, London EC4Y 0DZ, UK.

**Thunder Bay Press**
Publisher: Peter Norton
Associate Publisher: Ana Parker
Publishing/Editorial Team: April Farr, Kelly Larsen, Kathryn Chipinka, Aaron Guzman
Editorial Team: JoAnn Padgett, Melinda Allman, Dan Mansfield

Library of Congress Cataloging-in-Publication Data

Title: The Jim Beam bourbon cookbook.
Description: San Diego, California : Thunder Bay Press, [2017]
Identifiers: LCCN 2017034438 | ISBN 9781684120819 (hardcover)
Subjects: LCSH: Cooking (Whiskey) | Cocktails. | LCGFT: Cookbooks.
Classification: LCC TX726 .J57 2017 | DDC 641.6/2--dc23
LC record available at https://lccn.loc.gov/2017034438

Printed in China

21 20 19 18 17 1 2 3 4 5

# CONTENTS

# INTRODUCTION

# Any damn way you please.

*That's how we recommend you enjoy Jim Beam® bourbon—and that sentiment is shared by our master distiller, Fred Noe. And as a seventh-generation Beam, he should know.*

You see, Fred is passionate about all things bourbon. From the basic ingredients to the way it's distilled, right the way down to the specific method we use for charring our barrels to get that unique flavor that's made our bourbon number one in the world, enjoyed all over the globe.

And it's this unique flavor that's key in this book. Because although Jim Beam® makes for an undoubtedly fine drink on its own, it's when you begin to pair it with other ingredients that it can take you to a whole new level of taste.

Jim Beam® bourbon has an unmistakable flavor and aroma. It's bolder than other types of whiskey, with hints of smoke and caramel from our flame-charred barrels, and sweet vanilla notes that develop during the long years that it spends aging until it's ready to enjoy. Combine this with undertones of oak and spice inherent in any good bourbon, and you have a versatile ingredient that can bring a whole heap of taste to just about any dish.

We've spent long hours in our kitchens coming up with a collection of recipes that really makes the most of our bourbon. From quick and simple dishes that deliver on flavor but can be put together without much fuss, to some crowd-pleasing centerpieces that are sure to go down well at barbecues or parties, we've tried to cover every occasion.

So if you're looking for an indulgent treat for a special event, you can try the Eggs Benedict with Easy Bourbon Hollandaise on page 26, the Smoky Steak with Bourbon Butter on page 72, or the New York Bourbon Cheesecake on page 140. For something quick and easy that's packed with flavor, go for the Fully Loaded Black Bean Nachos on page 50 or the classic Kentucky Quarter Pounder on page 79. Or, if you're feeding a crowd, we've included some delicious recipes that you can scale up to suit your needs. Look no further than the Sticky Bourbon Wings with Asian Slaw on page 42 or the Pulled Pork Tacos with Sweetcorn Salsa on page 60.

And you'll be very pleased to hear that bourbon and chocolate are a killer combination. To get your sweet fix, turn to the Bourbon Cherry Brownies on page 122, the Easy Chocolate, Bourbon, and Raisin Ice Cream on page 148, or even the Kentucky Bourbon Chocolate Shake on page 150.

The beauty of all of these dishes—and the others in the book—is that they showcase the huge range of flavors that are enhanced with the addition of Jim Beam® bourbon. From light fish and shellfish to big, beautiful pieces of meat for roasting; from vegetables and sides to some truly decadent desserts, we've tried and tested them all, and collected the very greatest here for you to enjoy.

And, of course, no collection of Jim Beam® recipes would be complete without some cocktails. So, we've thought long and hard and brought together some of our absolute favorites. From stone-cold classics such as the Old Fashioned on page 176, to twists on some well-known drinks (check out the Kentucky Manhattan on page 174), there will be something here for everyone to enjoy.

So go ahead, flick through these pages, and bring the taste of Kentucky to your table. We guarantee you'll be pleased you did.

# HISTORY AND CHARACTER

# TWO CENTURIES OF BOURBON

For more than 200 years and through seven generations of the same family, we at Jim Beam have ensured that, in an ever-changing world, one thing remains constant, and that's the process of how we create our finest Kentucky Straight Bourbon Whiskey.

Our secret blend of corn, rye, and barley malt—known as our Mash Bill—is fed into a gigantic 10,000-gallon cooker. There, we add two crucial elements to the mix. The first is limestone-filtered Kentucky water, iron-free and rich in calcium, and the second is "setback"—some of the mash from the previous distillation.

We keep the content of our jug yeast secret, but it remains the same strain we've been using in our family business since the end of Prohibition in the 1930s. We mix the yeast with ground-up grain to create "dona yeast," which is then combined in the fermentation process, where the mash is cooled to 60–70°F. The yeast feeds on the sugars in the mash, creating carbon dioxide and, crucially, alcohol.

Next, we heat the mash (by now known as "distiller's beer" due to its similarity to beer in appearance, aroma, and taste) to 200°F in a 65-foot-tall column still, where it is vaporized and then liquidized. We go ahead and distill it for a second time in a doubler, where the vapor is condensed into something known as "high wine."

Once distillation has taken place, we make sure that this high wine is tapped into charred oak barrels, each of which can hold up to around 53 gallons, to age and mature into the bourbon that we know and love. While the barrels are kept in storage, the changeable climate of Kentucky results in the barrel wood expanding, then contracting. Bourbon seeps into the barrel while the charred wood produces sugars, rich in both color and flavor, with a caramelized taste. Meanwhile, some of the bourbon leaves the barrel through evaporation—we call the lost bourbon the "angel's share" or "Booker's share." The whole process takes up to four years, which is twice as long as the law requires.

Our familiar mellow, smooth Jim Beam® flavor, popular around the world, has been painstakingly developed and perfected since the late 18th century, thanks to seven hugely influential figures—all from the same family—who we now celebrate individually.

# THE SEVEN AGES OF BEAM

### Jacob Beam (1760–1834) "The Founder"

The origins of Jim Beam® whiskey stretch back to 1740, when the ambitious Boehm family arrived in the United States from Germany. The family changed their name to Beam, and by the 1770s the young Jacob Beam's father, Johannes, was one of the pioneering corn farmers in the Kentucky region of Virginia. In 1788, Jacob moved to central Kentucky, where a mild and warm climate and local limestone springs created the ideal conditions in which to grow corn. So much corn was grown that the excess was turned into whiskey, and in 1795, at the family distillery known as "Old Tub," Jacob sold his first barrel of "Old Jake Beam Sour Mash," made from his father's recipe. The new brand fast became a hit with pioneers, farmers, and traders.

### David Beam (1802–1854) "The Pioneer"

Even though Jacob Beam had established Old Jake Beam as a popular brand of bourbon, it was his son David who pioneered the brand's development. In 1820, David succeeded his father as the mastermind of the business, and under his watch the distillery expanded. More and more bourbon could be produced, as the distillery switched from the pot still to the more capacious column still, and as production increased, the extra bourbon could be transferred, by train or steamboat, to locations beyond the confines of Washington County. In 1830, the business began using the charred wood of oak barrels, which previously stored fish or vinegar, to produce the sugars for the now-famous caramelized taste of its bourbon.

### David M. Beam (1833–1913) "The Visionary"

When David M. Beam took over the business, he became aware of plans to extend railroad lines, and so in 1856 he moved the distillery to a location in Nelson County, which was practically next to the new tracks. As a result, the newly renamed D.M. Beam & Co. could transport its bourbon both north and south. The brand was rapidly gaining national acclaim, and by 1861, its quality and popularity had even reached presidential circles. After it became known that the Civil War general Ulysses S. Grant was an "avid bourbon consumer," his opponents confronted President Abraham Lincoln, accusing Grant of being a "drunkard." Lincoln reputedly responded: "Find out what he drinks and send a case to my other generals."

HISTORY AND CHARACTER

### Colonel James B. Beam (1864–1947) "The Colonel and the Legend"

It was James Beauregard Beam whose name would inspire the Jim Beam® brand. He took over the running of the distillery in 1894, by which time Old Tub® bourbon was well established as a national brand. Its secret recipe was of paramount importance, and Beam was protective of the contents of the yeast mix—he even took home a sample of the recipe to preserve the yeast strain. It is a strain that survives to this day. However, Beam's time running the distillery was interrupted in 1920 by Prohibition, and he abandoned the business. Fortunately for whiskey lovers everywhere, when the 18th Amendment was repealed in 1933, so ending Prohibition, Beam—now sixty-nine years old—began rebuilding the distillery in Clermont.

### T. Jeremiah Beam (1899–1977) "The Businessman"

It was James Beauregard Beam's son, T. Jeremiah, who helped him rebuild the distillery in 1933. They completed the task in just 120 days. By the time T. Jeremiah took over in 1946, not only had the revived Old Tub been renamed Jim Beam® Bourbon, but two new varieties had also become popular. Jim Beam® Rye was introduced in 1938, while the Mint Julep became the traditional drink of the Kentucky Derby. When he took charge, Beam initially oversaw the brand being shipped to U.S. servicemen overseas, insisting that no American should be without bourbon. To meet growing demand, a second distillery opened in Boston, Kentucky, in 1954.

### Fred Booker Noe II (1929–2004) "The Innovator"

Because Jim Beam's daughter Margaret had married into the Noe family, her son Booker Noe II would oversee the next era of Jim Beam®. He became master distiller at the Boston Booker Noe plant. By 1964, bourbon was recognized by Congress as the U.S. native spirit, and the following year, production reached one million barrels. Noe oversaw a number of significant developments in the Jim Beam® story. In 1978, Jim Beam Black® was introduced, and a decade later, Booker's small-batch Bourbon collection began to appear—handmade, uncut, and unfiltered, using Jim Beam family expertise to produce some of the world's finest bourbon.

### Frederick Booker Noe III (1957–) "The Global Ambassador"

Fred Booker Noe III is our current master distiller. Not only does he champion Jim Beam® all around the world, he is also charged with preserving our secret recipe, and ensuring that every batch of Jim Beam® has that same inimitable flavor. Prior to taking charge, Noe gained experience in all stages of the bourbon-making process, having begun his duties on the bottling line. He even grew up in the same house, in Bardstown, Kentucky, as his great-grandfather, Jim Beam himself. He is the custodian of the secrets of Jim Beam®—taking 200 years of bourbon-making history and distilling it into every single bottle of Jim Beam® Bourbon.

THE SEVEN AGES OF BEAM

# MEET THE FAMILY

The extended Jim Beam® family makes for quite a gathering—and every variety has a place in the kitchen. Though most of the recipes in this book are built around the classic taste of Jim Beam® Original, you can mix up the flavors in your dish by using different varieties of Jim Beam® Bourbon. From rich and full-bodied, to light and fruity, there is a variety to suit every taste, and to bring a different twist to many a dish.

### Jim Beam® Bourbon

This is the original. Made with a special blend of corn, rye, malted barley, water, time, and pride, Jim Beam® Original is the classic bourbon that people around the world know and love. A medium-bodied flavor, with mellow hints of caramel and vanilla, is reinforced by an oaky aroma with just a hint of spice. It's delicious, versatile, and a surefire crowd-pleaser. Use this in recipes for that classic, can't-be-beat bourbon flavor.

### Jim Beam Black® Bourbon

A smooth, elegant, refined drink, Jim Beam Black® Bourbon takes everything good about Jim Beam® Original Bourbon and turns it up a notch. Aged for years longer in white oak barrels, the flavors develop further to leave you with a full-bodied bourbon with a rich, heavy caramel flavor. An aroma of oak and vanilla lingers, with an undertone of cinnamon. This is the perfect partner for chocolate, or to finish off a dish with an extra punch.

## Jim Beam® Double Oak Bourbon
### finished in oak

Like all our bourbons, Jim Beam® Double Oak is developed in charred oak barrels. But its rich flavor comes from being aged a second time, in a separate barrel. The added interaction with the charred white oak results in a more intense bourbon, with toffee and caramel flavors, and rich notes of vanilla. Use this for barbecued meats, or to bring a light smokiness to cocktails.

## Jim Beam® Rye Whiskey

Founded in 1795, our rye whiskey is made in the pre-Prohibition style. With its spicy, warm flavor, underpinned by the particular fullness of rye, it brings a spicy kick to recipes, with a black pepper bite. It has hints of vanilla and oak, but isn't as sweet as traditional bourbon, so is better suited to savory dishes—though it can be used to tone down the sweetness of a dessert if you prefer a more savory flavor.

## Jim Beam® Apple
### Apple liqueur infused with bourbon

Infused with premium bourbon, this sweet apple liqueur is perfect
for bringing a light, sweet taste to a dish. Though underpinned
with a fresh, crisp, green apple flavor, it retains the subtle oak
undertones of bourbon. As you might expect, it works well in any
apple dessert, but it's also perfect in fruitier cocktails, and pairs
wonderfully with sweeter flavors such as maple syrup or honey.

## Jim Beam® Honey
### Honey liqueur infused with bourbon

One of the most versatile members of the Jim Beam® family, this is
a great bottle to have on hand in the kitchen. Made by taking real
golden honey liqueur and infusing it with our Kentucky Straight
Bourbon, it contains complex notes of caramel, oak, vanilla, and a
finish of sweet honey. It'll pair well with shellfish, is a great addition
to salad dressings, and brings out the best in meaty dishes.

## Jim Beam® Vanilla
## Vanilla liqueur infused with bourbon

Made by combining the natural flavor of Madagascar Bourbon Vanilla bean liqueur with our bourbon whiskey, Jim Beam®Vanilla has a beautiful balance of rich, full-bodied vanilla with subtle hints of oak, combined with deep, caramel notes. It's best to avoid using this in savory dishes, and instead focus on its ability to bring an added twist to fruity desserts, or any dish with chocolate.

## Red Stag by Jim Beam®
## Black cherry liqueur infused with bourbon

An infusion of black cherry liqueur with bourbon whiskey brings Red Stag by Jim Beam® a soft, dark black cherry aroma, backed with a traditional bourbon oak. Characterized by vanilla, oak, and caramel, its cherry sweetness is tempered by smooth bourbon notes. Warm and smooth, it's a great option for adding a fruity finish to a cocktail without overpowering the other ingredients.

MEET THE FAMILY

# APPETIZERS AND LIGHT BITES

# APPETIZERS AND LIGHT BITES

# Buttermilk Pancakes and Bacon with Bourbon Syrup

Give this classic breakfast dish an indulgent twist by making a sweet, sticky bourbon syrup to drizzle onto a stack of pancakes and smoky bacon. You'll be guaranteed to have folks lining up for a second helping—any time of day.

**SERVES 4**

**9 oz. (about 12 slices) smoked bacon**

For the bourbon syrup
**1 cup packed soft brown sugar**
**½ cup (1 stick) unsalted butter**
**¼ cup Jim Beam® Bourbon**

For the pancakes
**1½ cups all-purpose flour sifted
  with 1½ teaspoons baking powder**
**pinch of salt**
**2 tablespoons bourbon syrup
  (see above)**
**1 cup buttermilk, plus extra to
  loosen**
**1 large egg**
**3 teaspoons canola oil, divided**

★ Make the bourbon syrup first. Heat the sugar, butter, and bourbon in a small saucepan over medium heat until the mixture is bubbling, then immediately reduce the heat to the lowest setting and let simmer gently for 5 to 10 minutes. Remove from the heat and set aside. The mixture will thicken as it cools.

★ Preheat the broiler on a high setting. Broil the bacon for a few minutes on each side, until crisp.

★ To make the pancakes, add the flour and baking powder mixture to a wide, shallow bowl and stir through the salt. In a separate bowl, stir the 2 tablespoons of bourbon syrup into the buttermilk, then add the egg and whisk together well by hand. Pour the wet mixture into the flour mixture and gently combine, stirring as little as possible, to produce a thick, lumpy batter. Add a splash more buttermilk to loosen the batter.

★ You'll cook 12 pancakes in 3 batches, so select a suitably large nonstick skillet that will accommodate 4 pancakes simultaneously. Heat the skillet over medium-high heat and swirl 1 teaspoon oil across the bottom. Then add 4 separate spoonfuls of batter to the hot skillet and flatten them out. Cook for about 1 minute, until small holes appear across the surface of each pancake, then flip them over and cook for another minute, until cooked through. Transfer the pancakes to a warmed plate and keep them warm in the oven while you cook the remaining pancakes in the same way.

★ Serve each person 3 pancakes and 3 strips of bacon, drizzled with the cooled syrup to taste.

# Eggs Benedict with Easy Bourbon Hollandaise

Lacing a creamy hollandaise sauce with bourbon elevates eggs Benedict to a whole new level. Hollandaise has a reputation for being tricky to make, but have no fear—this recipe won't let you down. Just keep the heat low when cooking the egg yolks, and make sure you remove the mixture from the heat when you whisk in the butter. You can't go wrong!

**SERVES 4**

8 eggs

4 English muffins or bagels, split

butter, for spreading

5¾ oz. (at least 8 thin slices) good-quality cooked ham

1 teaspoon cayenne pepper

pepper

For the hollandaise sauce

3½ tablespoons Jim Beam® Bourbon

2 tablespoons white wine vinegar

2 shallots, minced

1 tablespoon water

2 egg yolks

½ cup plus 2 tablespoons (1¼ sticks) unsalted butter, melted and still warm

pinch of salt

★ To make the hollandaise sauce, put the bourbon, vinegar, shallots, and water into a small saucepan set over medium-low heat and let simmer for 2 to 3 minutes, until the liquid has reduced to less than one-third of the original quantity, so that 1 tablespoon of liquor remains. Strain the liquor into a medium-sized metal bowl, add the shallots to a separate bowl (to use as a garnish later), and set both aside.

★ Add water to a small saucepan until it is one-quarter full. Set it over medium heat and bring the water to a gentle simmer. Put the egg yolks into the metal bowl containing the liquor, set the bowl on the pan over the simmering water, and whisk the mixture continuously for 1 to 2 minutes, until frothy. Now remove the bowl from the heat and whisk briskly while pouring in the warm melted butter in a slow stream to thicken the sauce. Season with the salt and set aside.

★ To poach the eggs, bring a wide saucepan two-thirds full of water up to a simmer over medium heat. Stir with a spoon and then crack each egg into the water. Cook the eggs for 2 to 3 minutes, then drain on paper towels.

★ Meanwhile, toast the split muffins and spread with butter. Top each muffin half with ham, a poached egg, hollandaise sauce, and some shallots. Sprinkle with cayenne and pepper, and serve immediately.

# Butternut Squash Soup with Chili Peanuts

Bright and vibrant, this soup will warm the soul even on the coldest days. The chili peanuts with a spicy hint make a nice crunchy addition and, if you like, you can garnish the soup with a handful of chopped cilantro leaves for an extra splash of color and fresh taste.

**SERVES 4**

1 tablespoon sunflower or olive oil

2 tablespoons butter

1 onion, coarsely chopped

2 garlic cloves, minced or crushed

⅔ cup Jim Beam® Bourbon, plus 2 tablespoons to garnish, plus a splash extra as desired

1½ lb. butternut squash, peeled and chopped

½ teaspoon mild chili powder

3¼ cups vegetable or chicken stock, plus extra if needed

½ cup heavy cream

salt and pepper

For the chili peanuts

1 tablespoon sunflower or olive oil

2 tablespoons coarsely chopped unsalted peanuts

½ teaspoon mild chili powder

★ For the soup, heat the oil and butter in a Dutch oven or heavy saucepan set over medium heat. Add the onion and let fry for 5 minutes, until softened. Add the garlic and fry for 1 to 2 minutes, then pour in the bourbon and let the mixture simmer for 1 to 2 minutes. Stir in the butternut squash, chili powder, and stock. Bring to a boil, then let simmer, partially covered, for 20 to 25 minutes, or until the squash is completely tender.

★ Use a handheld stick blender to blend the mixture to a smooth consistency, adding a splash more stock or boiling water if you feel it is needed (if so, heat the soup again thoroughly after adding the extra stock or water). Stir in the cream and heat through. Season with salt and pepper. You can add another splash of Jim Beam® at this stage if you want more of a kick. Keep the soup warm.

★ For the chili peanuts, heat the oil in a skillet set over medium heat. Add the peanuts and fry for 2 to 3 minutes, until just lightly browned, then stir in the chili powder and cook for 1 minute.

★ Ladle the soup into warmed serving bowls and sprinkle with the chili peanuts. Return the pan to the heat and pour in the 2 tablespoons bourbon. Bring to a boil and let the bourbon bubble for 5 to 10 seconds, before removing from the heat. Swirl some hot bourbon over the surface of each serving of soup, and serve.

# Smoked Salmon with Pickled Vegetables

Pickling an assortment of vegetables in bourbon and pairing them with smoked salmon makes for an attractive and impressive appetizer. You can get creative with the vegetables you choose—whole fine asparagus, shaved fennel, ribbons of zucchini, sliced red onion, sliced radish, cubed carrot, or diced cucumber all work well. The pickled vegetables will keep well for a couple of days if stored in a sealed jar in the refrigerator.

### SERVES 4

3 tablespoons pine nuts

8 to 12 slices smoked salmon

For the pickling liquor

1 heaping tablespoon superfine sugar

1 tablespoon distilled vinegar

1½ tablespoons Jim Beam® Bourbon

½ heaping tablespoon fine table salt

1 tablespoon hot water

For the vegetables

1 small carrot, peeled and finely diced

1 small red onion, finely sliced

8 pink radishes, finely sliced

1 small zucchini, cut into ribbons with a vegetable peeler

8 fine asparagus stems

★ Mix all the ingredients for the pickling liquor in a bowl and whisk lightly to dissolve the sugar and salt. Add the vegetables and mix well. Refrigerate for a few hours, then drain the vegetables and dry them on paper towels.

★ Put the pine nuts into a small skillet set over low heat to toast gently for 2 to 3 minutes, until lightly golden. Set aside to cool.

★ Arrange 2 to 3 slices of smoked salmon on each plate. Top with a selection of the drained pickled vegetables and sprinkle with toasted pine nuts to serve.

# Spicy Shrimp Cocktail

Pimp your shrimp with this easy, spicy, bourbon-spiked sauce, which works beautifully with the subtle flavors of the shellfish. Served with a no-fuss crisp green salad and a big chunk of crusty bread to mop up the piquant sauce, this tasty Jim Beam® version of a retro dish makes for a fun start to any dinner party.

**SERVES 4**

1 crisp lettuce heart (such as little gem or romaine), sliced

1 avocado, cut into small chunks

10½ oz. cooked peeled jumbo shrimp

1 teaspoon cayenne pepper

pepper

crusty bread, to serve

For the sauce

⅓ cup Jim Beam® Bourbon

1 heaping tablespoon minced red onion

1 tablespoon soy sauce

½ tablespoon tomato paste

1 cup mayonnaise

½ to 1 teaspoon lemon juice

★ To make the sauce, put the bourbon, onion, and soy sauce into a small saucepan set over medium-low heat and let simmer for 4 to 5 minutes, or until 1 tablespoon of liquor remains. Mix in the tomato paste, stirring for 1 minute, then remove the pan from the heat. Pour the mixture into a bowl and set aside for a few minutes to cool to room temperature.

★ Add the mayonnaise to a bowl. Stir the cooled sauce mixture into the mayonnaise with lemon juice to taste.

★ Arrange the lettuce, avocado, and shrimp on a plate and drizzle with the sauce. Season with pepper and sprinkle with the cayenne pepper. Serve immediately with fresh crusty bread.

# Cobb Salad with Blue Cheese Bourbon Dressing

**SERVES 4**

A big, hearty Cobb salad is a guaranteed crowd-pleaser. Assemble the salad in the traditional style, layering the ingredients in rows on a platter, or throw it all together in a more casual mix.

For the bacon and grilled chicken

**1 tablespoon olive oil**

**2 teaspoons soy sauce**

**1 teaspoon Dijon mustard**

**1 garlic clove, crushed**

**2 boneless, skinless chicken breasts**

**8 slices smoked bacon**

**3 tablespoons Jim Beam® Bourbon**

**pepper**

For the blue cheese bourbon dressing

**¼ cup sour cream**

**¼ cup mayonnaise**

**2 teaspoons Dijon mustard**

**4½ oz. blue cheese (such as Roquefort), crumbled**

**2 tablespoons Jim Beam® Bourbon, plus extra to taste**

**1 garlic clove, crushed**

**salt and pepper**

For the salad

**1 large or 2 small heads of crisp lettuce (such as romaine), chopped**

**1 cup quartered or halved baby plum or cherry tomatoes**

**4 hard-boiled eggs, peeled and halved**

**4 scallions, thinly sliced**

**2 avocados, diced**

★ First prepare the bacon and grilled chicken. In a bowl, mix together the oil, soy sauce, mustard, garlic, and pepper. Add the chicken breasts and stir to coat. Set aside.

★ Heat a heavy skillet over medium-high heat and dry-fry the bacon for 2 to 3 minutes on each side, or until crisp and browned, then transfer to paper towels to drain. Add the chicken to the pan, reduce the heat to medium, and cook for 6 to 7 minutes on each side, or until browned and cooked through. Pour in the bourbon and let simmer for 1 to 2 minutes. Then turn off the heat and let cool.

★ To make the dressing, mix all the ingredients together in a bowl or pitcher, season with salt and pepper, and add more bourbon to taste, if desired.

★ Assemble the salad ingredients either on a large platter or in individual bowls. Break the bacon into small pieces and arrange them on top of the salad. Cut the cold chicken into strips or cubes, toss in any pan juices, and arrange the chicken next to the bacon. Serve immediately, with the dressing on the side, or drizzled on top.

# Watercress and Feta Salad with Honey Dressing

The smoky-sweet flavor of Jim Beam® Honey works superbly with the saltiness of feta cheese, and the combination is even better when finished with a little kick of mustard and red chili. This recipe makes a perfect vegetarian light meal for four, but it's also great served on the side at a barbecue. Wait until the last minute to prepare and add the avocado, then drizzle with the dressing.

**SERVES 4**

For the dressing

⅔ **cup Jim Beam® Honey**

**zest and juice of 2 oranges**

**1 tablespoon liquid honey**

**2 tablespoons whole-grain mustard**

**2 teaspoons apple cider vinegar**

**2 hot red chilies, finely sliced**

¼ **cup canola oil**

**salt and pepper**

For the salad

**7 oz. watercress, washed**

9¼ **oz. feta cheese**

**2 avocados, sliced**

¼ **cup chopped roasted hazelnuts**

★ To make the dressing, place the bourbon, orange juice, and orange zest in a small saucepan set over medium heat and let simmer for 5 to 10 minutes, until the smell of the alcohol has disappeared.

★ Pour this mixture into a large jam jar, add the remaining dressing ingredients, seal securely with the lid, and shake well to combine. Taste and adjust the seasoning, if necessary, then set aside to cool.

★ Divide the watercress equally among 4 plates, then sprinkle with crumbled chunks of feta cheese. Add slices of avocado and drizzle with the dressing. Finish each plate with a tablespoon of chopped hazelnuts.

# Warm Chicken Caesar Salad

Try this warm and wintery take on the classic chicken Caesar salad. Once you try the bourbon-laced chicken breasts, it'll be hard to make them any other way ever again. Luckily, you won't need to, because they're incredibly versatile. Just add them to any green salad to bring a smoky bourbon flavor to your dish.

**SERVES 4**

For the croutons

**7 oz. ciabatta, torn into bite-size pieces**

**1 tablespoon Jim Beam® Bourbon**

**3 tablespoons canola oil**

**3 large boneless, skinless chicken breasts**

**1 tablespoon canola oil**

**½ cup Jim Beam® Bourbon**

**7 oz. kale, sliced**

**2¼ oz. Parmesan cheese, cut into shavings using a vegetable peeler**

**¼ cup Caesar dressing**

**salt and pepper**

★ Preheat the oven and a nonstick baking pan to 350°F.

★ To make the croutons, first put the chunks of ciabatta into a bowl. Pour the bourbon and oil into a small jar with a lid, seal securely, and shake well to blend. Then pour the mixture over the bread and squeeze it into the chunks by hand. Put the bread into the preheated pan and bake for 12 to 18 minutes, until the croutons begin to turn golden.

★ Place the chicken breasts on a piece of plastic wrap and cover with a second piece. Using a rolling pin or mallet, pound the meat to flatten it to an even thickness of about ½ inch. Season both sides of each flattened chicken breast with salt and pepper.

★ Select a large nonstick skillet that has a lid, add the oil, and set over high heat. Add the chicken and brown for about 3 minutes on each side. Pour in the bourbon and let it bubble for 2 to 4 minutes, then reduce the heat to the lowest setting, cover the pan with the lid, and cook for 5 to 8 minutes until the chicken is cooked through. Switch off the heat and let rest.

★ Place the chicken and all of the pan juices into a wide, shallow bowl. Using 2 forks, shred the chicken into the juice.

★ Meanwhile, return the pan to the stove over high heat, add the kale, cover, and let cook for 3 to 5 minutes, until the leaves have wilted and most of the moisture has evaporated.

★ Layer the warm kale, Parmesan shavings, croutons, and chicken onto warmed plates, drizzle with the Caesar dressing, and serve.

# Jim Beam® Chicken Nuggets

A time-honored sharing dish, chicken nuggets have a place on any table. In this recipe, the nuggets are marinated in bourbon before they're baked on low heat, ensuring that the final dish stays moist and flavorsome. Serve with ketchup for dipping, or try the Bourbon Barbecue Dip on page 111.

**SERVES 4**

1¼ lb. boneless, skinless chicken
  breasts, cut into chunks

¼ cup all-purpose flour

2 small eggs, lightly beaten

1 cup fine dry bread crumbs

spray oil

ketchup, to serve

For the marinade

⅔ cup Jim Beam® Bourbon

1½ teaspoons soy sauce

★ To make the marinade, heat the bourbon in a small saucepan and simmer for 2 minutes, then stir in the soy sauce. Set aside to cool completely.

★ Place the chicken pieces in a wide, shallow bowl. Add the cooled marinade and toss to coat the chicken pieces thoroughly. Cover the bowl with plastic wrap and refrigerate for 2 hours.

★ Preheat the oven and a nonstick baking pan to 325°F.

★ Remove the chicken from the refrigerator and discard the marinade. Place the chicken onto a plate lined with paper towels and pat with more paper towels repeatedly until each piece is thoroughly dry.

★ Put the flour, eggs, and bread crumbs into 3 separate wide, shallow bowls. Dip each piece of chicken first into the flour, then shake off any excess. Next, dip it into the beaten egg. Finally, roll it in the bread crumbs to coat.

★ Spray the preheated baking pan with a little oil. Arrange the coated chicken pieces on the pan and spray each piece with a little oil. Bake for 15 minutes, then increase the oven temperature to 350°F and bake for another 5 minutes, or until golden. Serve with ketchup.

# Sticky Bourbon Wings with Asian Slaw

These tasty chicken wings are an irresistible snack, and the recipe is easily doubled or even tripled if you're feeding a crowd at a get-together. Fingers will get messy here, so a stack of napkins when you serve up is a must! Be sure to shred and slice the slaw ingredients as thinly as you can (you may want to use a food processor for this) to get a really fresh, crunchy effect.

**SERVES 4**

For the Asian slaw

**1 cup grated carrot**

**1½ cups finely shredded white cabbage**

**1 small red onion, finely sliced into half moons**

**10 sprigs of cilantro, leaves stripped**

**juice of 1 lime**

For the wings

**2 tablespoons Jim Beam® Bourbon**

**¼ cup sweet chili sauce**

**20 chicken wings**

**1 to 2 tablespoons peanut oil**

**salt and pepper**

★ Preheat the oven to 500°F.

★ Stir the slaw ingredients together thoroughly to combine in a bowl and set aside in the refrigerator until needed.

★ To prepare the wings, first mix the bourbon with the sweet chili sauce in a bowl.

★ Pat the chicken wings repeatedly with paper towels to dry them thoroughly, then coat well with the oil and arrange in a single layer on a large baking pan. Roast for 30 minutes.

★ Using a metal spatula, gently release the chicken wings from the baking pan where they are sticking, then stir the bourbon and sweet chili mixture into the baking pan to coat all the wings. Season with salt and pepper, then roast for another 5 to 10 minutes, stirring halfway through, until the sauce is thick and sticky and the chicken skin blackens in places. Serve with the slaw.

# Jim Beam® Piri Piri Shrimp Skewers

The light flavor of Jim Beam® Honey pairs perfectly with sweet shrimp and spicy piri piri sauce, but this recipe works just as well when made with Jim Beam® Bourbon. The marinated shrimp are also delicious served cold on a simple salad.

**SERVES 4**

14 oz. raw, peeled (or with just tails) jumbo shrimp, defrosted if frozen

⅓ cup piri piri sauce

2 tablespoons Jim Beam® Honey

1 tablespoon peanut oil

pepper

To serve

1 fennel bulb, finely sliced or shredded using a mandoline slicer

¼ cup lemon juice

1 lemon, quartered into wedges

★ If using wooden skewers, soak them in cold water for 30 minutes before using.

★ Pat the shrimp with paper towels to dry them thoroughly.

★ Mix the piri piri sauce and bourbon together in a bowl, add the shrimp, mix well, and refrigerate for an hour or so to marinate.

★ Combine the fennel with the lemon juice in a bowl and set aside.

★ Prepare a barbecue to allow you to cook over high heat, or set a griddle pan on your stove over high heat.

★ Divide the shrimp equally among the skewers and thread each shrimp onto the skewer through both the tail and the body to prevent them from twisting. Brush each of the skewered shrimp with oil and some of the marinade, and then season each side of the shrimp with pepper.

★ Put the skewers onto the barbecue or griddle pan and cook for 2 to 3 minutes on each side, depending on their size, until all of the gray flesh has turned pink. Brush the skewers with more marinade as they cook.

★ Divide the skewers into 4 equal portions and serve with some fennel salad and a lemon wedge.

# Shrimp Burgers with Bourbon Mayonnaise

This is a sweet-and-spicy snack that can be whipped up without much notice. You can use the shrimp straight from the freezer, since they defrost so quickly. To turn it into a more substantial meal, serve with homemade sweet potato chips and extra mayonnaise on the side for dipping, or Potato Wedges with Bourbon Barbecue Dip (see page 111).

**SERVES 4**

½ cup Jim Beam® Bourbon

3 shallots, minced

1½ teaspoons soy sauce

½ cup mayonnaise

1 lb. 2 oz. raw shelled jumbo shrimp, defrosted if frozen

1 small garlic clove

pinch of salt

1 hot red chili, finely sliced

4 brioche burger buns, split

2 teaspoons canola oil

handful of peppery lettuce leaves (such as arugula)

★ Put the bourbon, shallots, and soy sauce into a small saucepan. Bring the mixture to a boil, then let boil for 2 to 3 minutes. Remove the pan from the heat and set aside to cool, then divide the mixture into 2 equal portions. Combine one portion with the mayonnaise and set this aside. Set aside the remaining portion.

★ Place the raw shrimp in a food processor with the garlic and a pinch of salt and pulse a few times until the mixture is coarsely combined. Tip it into a bowl and stir in the remaining cooled bourbon-and-shallot mixture and the chili.

★ Divide this mixture into 4 equal portions. With wet hands, shape each portion into a patty. The mixture may seem wet and sticky, but it will firm up while cooking.

★ Toast the brioche buns lightly, then let cool.

★ Put the oil into a large nonstick skillet that has a lid and heat it over high heat. Add the patties and fry for 3 minutes on each side. Now reduce the heat to low, cover the pan with the lid, and cook for another minute.

★ While you are cooking the patties, spread the toasted buns with the seasoned mayonnaise. Once the patties are cooked, place one on the lower half of each bun. Divide the lettuce leaves into 4 portions and arrange on top of the patty in each bun, cover with the top half of the bun, and serve immediately.

# Fully Loaded Black Bean Nachos

Jim Beam® Bourbon adds just the right amount of smokiness to this easy black bean topping, which is always a hit piled onto a big plate of nachos and smothered with cheese. This is the perfect snack to serve up while spending time with friends and family, and meat lovers won't even notice it is vegetarian. (Shown on previous page.)

**SERVES 4**

7 oz. salted tortilla chips

¼ cup sliced jalapeño peppers from a jar, drained

5½ oz. of your favorite cheese for melting (such as Monterey Jack or Gouda), grated

½ cup sour cream, to serve

For the black bean topping

1 tablespoon canola oil

1 red onion, cut into thin wedges

½ teaspoon cumin seeds

1 fat garlic clove, minced

pinch of salt

5 cherry tomatoes, halved

1 teaspoon chili powder

3 tablespoons Jim Beam® Bourbon

14-oz. can black beans, drained and rinsed

pinch of dried oregano (optional)

★ To make the topping, mix the oil, onion, cumin seeds, garlic, and salt in a small, cold, nonstick skillet. Then set the pan over medium-low heat. Cook gently for about 7 minutes, or until the onion is soft. Stir in the tomatoes and let cook for another 3 minutes, then mix in the chili powder.

★ Increase the heat to medium, pour in the bourbon along with a splash of water, and let boil for 1 minute. Then add the black beans and simmer for 5 to 10 minutes. Now stir in the oregano, if using.

★ Preheat the oven to 400°F, or the broiler to a high setting.

★ Arrange the tortilla chips in an ovenproof dish and top with the black bean mixture, followed by the sliced jalapeño peppers. Sprinkle with the grated cheese. Bake or broil until the cheese has melted. Serve immediately, with dollops of sour cream.

# Hot Dogs with Onion Chutney

This bourbon onion chutney is quick to make, but it's not for the fainthearted. It's supercharged with bourbon, chili flakes, and pepper, and is best served warm, smothered over your favorite hot dogs. Don't expect any leftovers! (Shown on next page.)

**SERVES 4**

For the bourbon onion chutney

**1 tablespoon canola oil**

**¾ lb. red onions, sliced into half moons**

**1 teaspoon sea salt flakes**

**1 teaspoon yellow mustard seeds**

**½ teaspoon dried red chili flakes**

**3 tablespoons soft brown sugar**

**3 tablespoons Jim Beam® Bourbon**

**3 tablespoons apple cider vinegar**

**pepper**

For the hot dogs

**4 large hot dogs**

**2 tablespoons of your favorite mustard**

**4 large hot dog buns, split**

★ Pour the oil into a large nonstick skillet. Add the onions and thoroughly coat the slices in the oil. Set the pan over medium heat. Once sizzling, stir in the salt, mustard seeds, chili flakes, and plenty of pepper. Cook for 5 to 10 minutes, until the onions are soft.

★ Reduce the heat to low, stir in the sugar, and cook for 5 minutes to allow the sugar to melt into the mixture. Then increase the heat to medium, stir in the bourbon and vinegar, and cook for 5 minutes or until the liquid evaporates. Switch off the heat.

★ Meanwhile, cook the hot dogs following the package directions. Spread ½ tablespoon mustard over each bun and add a hot dog. Top with the warm bourbon onion chutney and serve immediately.

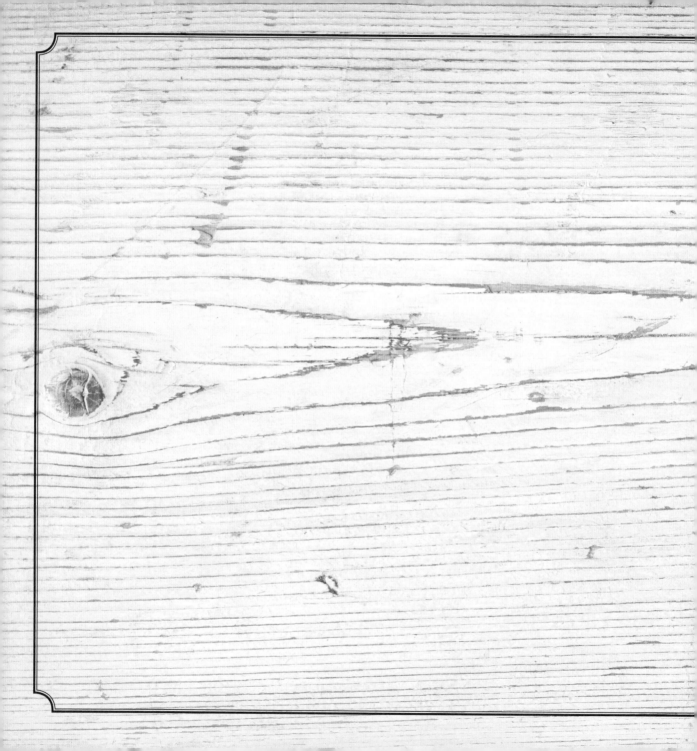

# MAIN COURSES

# MAIN COURSES

# Pork Chops with Creamy Bourbon Mushrooms

This dish makes something a little indulgent from the humble pork chop. Served with a creamy mushroom and bourbon sauce, it is perfect for a weekday evening meal. Add plenty of green vegetables and mashed potatoes to create a hearty dinner.

**SERVES 4**

4 pork chops, each 1 inch thick (total weight approximately 2 lb.)

1 tablespoon canola oil

4 shallots, sliced

1¼ lb. mushrooms

½ cup Jim Beam® Bourbon

⅓ to ½ cup heavy cream

salt and pepper

★ Preheat the oven to 350°F. Set a large nonstick skillet over medium-high heat.

★ Brush the chops with the oil and season well with salt and pepper. Put them into the hot skillet and cook for 5 minutes on each side, disturbing them only to turn them over once.

★ Transfer the chops to a roasting pan and roast for 10 minutes until cooked. Remove from the oven and let rest for a few minutes.

★ Meanwhile, make the sauce. Reduce the heat under the skillet to medium and add the shallots to the pan. Fry for 1 minute, then add the mushrooms and stir to coat in the rendered pork fat. Season with salt and pepper. Add the bourbon and let cook until the chops are nearly ready to come out of the oven. Reduce the heat to low and stir in the cream.

★ Serve each pork chop on a warmed plate, covered with the mushroom and bourbon sauce.

# Pulled Pork Tacos with Sweet Corn Salsa

A shoulder cut is traditionally used for pulled pork, but braising pork belly slowly in liquor creates sublime results because the meat just falls apart into the rich cooking stock. This dish tastes even better made ahead and served the next day. Simply reheat it gently in a saucepan with a little water.

**SERVES 4**

1 tablespoon cumin seeds

1 tablespoon olive oil

1 red onion, coarsely cut into wedges

⅓ cup soy sauce

3 tablespoons Jim Beam® Bourbon

2 tablespoons maple syrup

1¼ cups water, plus extra as required

2¾ lb. pork belly, skin removed, cut into 8 pieces as bones allow (reserve the bones)

12 soft or hard taco shells

For the sweet corn salsa

1 cup drained canned corn kernels

½ red onion, minced

1 red chili, finely diced

1 small bunch of cilantro, leaves and stems finely chopped

juice of 1 lime

★ Preheat the oven to 350°F.

★ Heat a small Dutch oven over medium heat, add the cumin seeds, and toast for just 2 minutes, until fragrant. Add the oil and onion and cook for 5 minutes, until the onion is soft.

★ Switch off the heat, add the soy sauce, bourbon, maple syrup, and measured water and stir to combine. Now add the pork belly pieces, ensuring they are submerged in the liquid. Cover the Dutch oven with the lid. You need a tight fit here to really lock the flavors into the pot, so if the lid fits the pot loosely, wrap the lid in aluminum foil before settting it onto the pot.

★ Transfer to the oven and cook for 4 hours, checking every hour or so and adding a little more water if necessary. Remove from the oven and let rest, covered, for 30 minutes.

★ Meanwhile, mix all the salsa ingredients together in a bowl.

★ When the pork has rested, discard any liquid fat from the surface and remove all bones and any large chunks of fat. Using 2 forks, pull the meat into the remaining sauce and add a splash of water to loosen.

★ Warm the tacos following the package directions.

★ Serve the warm meat inside the tacos, topped with the sweet corn salsa.

# Bourbon and Bacon Risotto

Traditionally, risotto is made with white wine, but for a simple twist, replace the wine with a good splash of bourbon. The results are delicious! As with any risotto, you'll need to stir the rice patiently throughout cooking, but the end result is rich and creamy, and well worth the time spent at the stove.

❖ ⟡ ❖

**SERVES 4**

5 cups chicken stock

2 tablespoons canola oil

4 shallots, minced

4 garlic cloves, minced

4 celery stalks, finely chopped

10½ oz. smoked bacon, finely chopped

1½ cups risotto rice

¾ cup Jim Beam® Bourbon

¾ cup Parmesan cheese, grated

handful of chives, snipped

3 tablespoons unsalted butter, cut into small cubes

pepper

★ Heat the stock in a saucepan and keep it at a low simmer.

★ Put the oil into a large, shallow, heavy saucepan set over low heat. Add the shallots, garlic, and celery and cook gently for about 5 minutes, until soft. Increase the heat to medium, stir in the bacon, and cook for a few minutes, until the bacon is cooked.

★ Add the rice and stir for about 3 minutes to heat the grains. Add the bourbon and stir until it has cooked away. Now add a ladleful of the stock and cook until all the liquid has been absorbed by the rice. Continue adding the stock, a ladleful at a time, ensuring all the liquid is absorbed by the rice between additions, until all the stock has been added. This should take 20 to 30 minutes. Add another 1 or 2 ladles of water if the rice is not yet tender, and cook until absorbed.

★ Stir in the Parmesan, chives, and butter and serve immediately on warmed plates with some freshly ground black pepper.

# Bourbon Baby Back Ribs

This sauce is a marinade, cooking sauce, and glaze all in one, so all of the awesome flavor is carried right through to the final dish. It's definitely worth marinating the meat if you have the time, but if you need a quick fix, you can skip this stage. Cook the meat in the oven, then finish it on the barbecue, if you can, for the ultimate rack of ribs.
(Shown on pages 66–67.)

**SERVES 4**

3¼ lb. or 3 racks of pork

½ cup tomato ketchup

For the marinade

3 tablespoons Jim Beam® Bourbon

3 tablespoons dark soy sauce

2 tablespoons balsamic vinegar

2 tablespoons dark brown sugar

½ tablespoon tomato paste

1 teaspoon ground cumin

½ teaspoon mustard powder

¼ teaspoon smoked paprika

★ Mix the marinade ingredients together in a small saucepan set over medium-low heat and simmer for 3 to 5 minutes. Set aside to cool completely.

★ Remove the thin membrane from the underside of each rack of pork and discard it.

★ Place one large food bag inside another to create a double layer. Add the ribs and marinade, squeeze out the air, and seal the bags. Marinate the meat in the refrigerator for approximately 4 hours, turning the bag over occasionally.

★ When ready to cook, preheat the oven to 350°F. Place the ribs and all of the sauce into a large roasting pan, cover tightly with aluminum foil, and roast for 1½ hours.

★ If you are finishing the dish on the barbecue, prepare the barbecue so that you can cook over high heat.

★ Once the cooking time has elapsed, remove the meat from the roasting pan and set it aside to rest while thickening the sauce. Place the pan on the stove over high heat, stir in the ketchup, and let boil for 3 to 5 minutes, until thick.

★ If you are finishing off the meat in the oven, increase the oven temperature to 400°F. Return the meat to the pan and brush it with the thickened glaze from the pan. Return the pan to the oven and cook, uncovered, for another 10 to 15 minutes or until the meat is done to your liking.

★ If charring on the barbecue, brush the racks with the glaze, place them on the barbecue, and cook for at least 10 minutes, brushing the thick glaze over the ribs repeatedly while barbecuing.

# Beam's Baked Ham

A glorious centerpiece for any gathering, this baked ham is slow-roasted with bourbon liquor and then glazed with the bourbon cooking juices to give it a dark and delicious crust.

**SERVES 4 TO 6**

3¼ lb. smoked boneless ham

⅔ cup Jim Beam® Honey, plus extra as required

1 heaping tablespoon whole-grain mustard

1 teaspoon liquid honey

½ to 1 teaspoon chili powder

★ When buying your ham, check whether or not it needs soaking prior to cooking. If it does, submerge it in water in a large bowl and refrigerate for 24 hours. Drain the ham.

★ Preheat the oven to 350°F.

★ Place the ham in a roasting dish so that it fits snugly. Pour the bourbon into the dish around the ham, and cover the dish with a large piece of aluminum foil in one direction, pinching the edges of the foil together. Then use a second piece of foil to cover the ham in the other direction in the same way.

★ Cook for 4 hours, checking it from time to time. If the roasting dish becomes dry during cooking, add another splash of bourbon.

★ Remove the ham from the dish. Pour the cooking juices into a small gravy boat, diluting with a splash of water if very salty, and reserve. Carefully remove just the skin from the ham, leaving on as much fat as possible. Score the fat with a widely spaced criss-cross pattern. Increase the oven temperature to 425°F. Return the ham to the roasting dish.

★ Mix the mustard, honey, and chili powder together in a small bowl. Spoon one-third of this mixture onto the top of the ham and roast, uncovered, for 30 minutes, applying more glaze every 10 minutes. Let the ham rest for 15 minutes, then serve with a little of the warmed roasting juices.

# Spiked Chili Con Carne

Bourbon brings a whole new dimension to this crowd-pleasing dinner, and if you haven't tried adding a little dark chocolate to a chili, then you really need to give this recipe a try. It may sound odd, but just give it a try—it adds a delicious richness. Serve with a dollop of sour cream, with rice or Bourbon Cornbread with Chili Flakes (see page 114) alongside.

**SERVES 4**

1 heaping teaspoon cumin seeds

2 tablespoons canola oil

2 red onions, chopped

pinch of salt

1¾ lb. ground beef

2 tablespoons tomato paste

1 to 2 teaspoons chili powder

½ teaspoon sweet smoked paprika

¾ cup Jim Beam® Bourbon

14-oz. can diced tomatoes

1¼ cups beef stock

1¾ cups water

14-oz. can kidney beans, drained

¾ oz. dark chocolate, broken into pieces (optional)

salt and pepper

★ Heat a large Dutch oven over medium-high heat, then add the cumin seeds and toast for 1 to 2 minutes, until they release their fragrance. Then add the oil, onions, and salt and fry for 5 minutes or until the onions are soft.

★ Add the ground beef, season it with salt and pepper, and cook until the meat begins to brown and the moisture from the ground beef evaporates. Stir in the tomato paste, chili powder, and smoked paprika and cook for another 2 minutes.

★ Preheat the oven to 350°F.

★ Pour the bourbon into the Dutch oven and cook for 3 minutes, then stir in the canned tomatoes, beef stock, measured water, and kidney beans, then bring the mixture to a simmer. Cover the Dutch oven with the lid, transfer to the oven, and cook for 2 hours.

★ Remove the Dutch oven from the oven and stir in the chocolate, if using. Serve in warmed bowls with your favorite accompaniments, such as rice, lime wedges, and sour cream.

# Smoky Steak with Bourbon Butter

Try this dish for an awesome combination of flavors and the ultimate way to prepare a steak. You can make it indoors on a griddle pan or outdoors on the barbecue, but during cooking make sure you give each steak enough space (cook in batches if necessary). The delicious bourbon butter is all you need on the side.

**SERVES 4**

**4 of your favorite type of steak, at room temperature**

For the bourbon butter

**¼ cup (½ stick) slightly salted butter, at room temperature**

**1 teaspoon mustard powder**

**1 tablespoon Jim Beam® Bourbon**

For the smoky paste

**1½ teaspoons sweet smoked paprika**

**1½ teaspoons sea salt flakes**

**2 tablespoons peanut oil**

**pepper**

★ To make the bourbon butter, mash the butter with a fork until it is smooth, then mix in the mustard powder and bourbon and set aside.

★ Combine all the smoky paste ingredients in a shallow bowl and season with plenty of pepper. Set the steaks on a plate or platter and thoroughly coat each steak with the paste.

★ Prepare the barbecue to cook over the highest heat or set a griddle pan over high heat. Sear the steaks on each side until cooked to your liking.

★ Smear or baste both sides of the steaks liberally with the bourbon butter. Let the steaks rest for 5 minutes, then top with any remaining butter to serve.

# Barbecue Bourbon and Harissa Beef

A good-quality fillet of beef speaks for itself, but this ultra-quick marinade will bring out the very best in your meat, adding a hint of smokiness and a lick of spice from the harissa. Cook the meat on the barbecue to your liking, and serve it with some simple green vegetables.

**SERVES 4**

¾ cup Jim Beam® Bourbon
3 tablespoons harissa
1¾ lb. fillet of beef

★ Put the bourbon into a small saucepan, bring it to a boil, then simmer for 7 to 10 minutes or until reduced to a little more than 3 tablespoons. Mix in the harissa and set aside to cool a little.

★ Place the beef fillet in a plastic food bag and pour in the marinade. Squeeze the air out of the bag, then seal it. Set aside at room temperature for 1 hour, squeezing the bag now and again to help the marinade penetrate the meat.

★ Prepare the barbecue to allow you to cook over medium-high heat. Sear the beef for 1 to 2 minutes on all sides (about 8 minutes in total). Then reduce the heat of the barbecue by dispersing the coals a little, or by selecting a medium setting on a gas barbecue. Cover with the lid, and cook until the meat is done to your liking, turning it over halfway through cooking time. The exact length of time needed will depend on the temperature of the barbecue and the thickness of the beef, but as an approximate guide, cook for an additional 2 to 3 minutes for rare, 3 minutes for medium-rare, and 4 minutes for medium.

★ Cover the meat loosely with aluminum foil and let rest for 10 minutes before serving.

# Slow-Cooked Whiskey Brisket

Homely and comforting, this dish is ideal for feeding a crowd. The recipe produces a rich bourbon gravy and a pile of buttered mashed potatoes. The potatoes are baked in the oven alongside the brisket, so are easy to make. It's definitely worth letting the brisket rest for about 30 minutes once it's out of the oven, to ensure the meat retains the delicious juices.

**SERVES 4 GENEROUSLY**

2¾-lb. piece of beef brisket, boned, rolled, and tied

2 tablespoons canola oil

4 shallots, sliced

4 garlic cloves, crushed

¾ lb. carrots, quartered lengthwise, then diced

2 celery stalks, halved lengthwise, then thinly sliced

1½ tablespoons all-purpose flour

⅔ cup Jim Beam® Bourbon, plus extra to taste

2 cups beef stock

½ to 1 tablespoon dark soy sauce

2 bay leaves

2 sprigs of rosemary

1¾ cups water

sea salt flakes and pepper

For the mashed potatoes

6 baking potatoes (such as russet), skins pierced with a sharp knife

⅔ cup milk

2 tablespoons unsalted butter

sea salt

★ Remove the brisket from the refrigerator and let rest for 1 hour to bring it to room temperature. Pat the meat dry with paper towels and season with salt and pepper. Preheat the oven to 350°F.

★ Set a medium-size Dutch oven over high heat and add the oil. When the oil is hot, add the brisket and brown it on all sides for about 15 minutes, then remove it from the Dutch oven and set aside.

Continued on next page ⟶

★ Reduce the heat to low. Add the shallots and garlic with a tiny pinch of salt and fry for 3 minutes, until they begin to soften. Now add the carrots and celery and cook for 3 minutes, then mix in the flour and cook for another 2 minutes. Stir in the bourbon, increase the heat to medium, bring the mixture to a boil, and boil for 2 minutes. Add the stock, soy sauce to taste, fresh herbs, and half the measured water and bring to a simmer.

★ Place the brisket back into the Dutch oven and cover tightly with the lid. Transfer to the oven and let cook for 4½ hours, stirring occasionally.

★ After half of the cooking time has elapsed, put the potatoes into the oven, placing them directly onto the oven rack.

★ After the cooking time has elapsed, remove the Dutch oven from the oven, lift out the meat, and transfer it to a board. Cover loosely with aluminum foil and let rest while you make the gravy and mashed potatoes.

★ Place the Dutch oven on the stove over high heat and add a few more splashes of bourbon, if you like, along with the remaining measured water. Remove any woody herbs and simmer the gravy briskly until it has reduced to your liking.

★ For the mashed potatoes, warm the milk and butter in a large saucepan. Meanwhile, wearing oven mitts, cut each potato in half and scoop out the flesh into the warm milk and butter mixture. Stir well and season with salt.

★ Slice the brisket and pour any resting juices into the gravy. Serve on warmed plates with the mashed potatoes and lots of gravy.

# Kentucky Quarter Pounder

This is an indulgent bourbon-spiked twist on the classic burger, complete with meltingly soft bourbon onions. Top it with cheese in a brioche bun and serve with skinny fries for a whole new way of enjoying a satisfying quarter pounder. (Shown on the next page.)

**SERVES 4**

For the burgers

**1 lb. ground round or ground sirloin**

**¼ cup fine dry bread crumbs**

**1 small egg, lightly beaten**

**1½ tablespoons Jim Beam® Bourbon**

**½ to 1 tablespoon oil (if needed)**

**4 slices of your favorite cheese for melting (such as Monterey Jack or Gouda)**

**salt and pepper**

For the bourbon onions

**1 tablespoon unsalted butter**

**1 tablespoon canola oil**

**2 white onions, sliced into half moons**

**2 to 3 tablespoons Jim Beam® Bourbon**

To serve

**4 brioche burger buns, split**

**shredded crunchy lettuce**

**ketchup and mayonnaise (optional)**

★ To make the burgers, add the ground beef, bread crumbs, egg, and bourbon to a bowl, mixing thoroughly by hand to combine. Divide the mixture into 4 equal portions and shape each portion into a patty. Season both sides with salt and pepper and set aside to rest.

★ Now make the bourbon onions. Heat a nonstick skillet over medium-high heat and melt the butter with the oil. Once frothy, add the onions and cook for 10 minutes, stirring occasionally, until soft. Add the bourbon and continue to cook until the onion slices are thickly coated and golden. Remove them from the pan with a slotted spoon and set aside.

★ Return the pan to the stove over high heat to cook the patties. Add the oil, if necessary, and cook the patties for 3 minutes on one side. Then flip them over once again and set a slice of cheese on top of each. Cook for another 3 minutes, until the cheese begins to melt. Remove the patties from the pan and set aside to rest for 2 minutes.

★ While the patties rest, return the onions to the pan to heat through and gather flavor. Meanwhile, toast the buns.

★ To serve, make a stack on the lower half of each bun with lettuce, a patty, and onions, then set the remaining bun half on top.

# Barbecued Lamb Skewers

Don't let the anchovy in this marinade worry you. It adds a deep saltiness that blends beautifully with the marinade flavors, and by the time the lamb is cooked there will be no hint of the fishiness at all. These skewers are great served with flatbread to soak up all the lovely juices, with a crisp, crunchy salad on the side.

## SERVES 4

¾ cup Jim Beam® Bourbon

3 garlic cloves, crushed

2 sprigs of rosemary, leaves stripped

1 tablespoon balsamic vinegar

1 small anchovy fillet, chopped

½ tablespoon canola oil

1½ lb. leg of lamb, cut into chunks

1 large red onion, cut into small wedges

pepper

To serve

4 pieces of flatbread

crisp salad

★ Pour the bourbon into a small saucepan and bring to a boil, then simmer for 7 to 10 minutes or until reduced to a little over 3 tablespoons.

★ Reduce the heat to medium and add the garlic, rosemary leaves, balsamic vinegar, and anchovy and let simmer, stirring continuously, for about 3 minutes. Remove the pan from the heat, stir in the oil and some pepper, then set aside to cool a little.

★ Place the chunks of lamb into a bowl so that they fit snugly, and pour the cooled mixture evenly over the meat. Transfer the bowl to the refrigerator to marinate for about 1 hour, stirring the meat in the marinade once or twice.

★ Prepare the barbecue for direct cooking over medium heat.

★ Thread the marinated chunks of lamb onto 8 metal skewers, alternating chunks of meat with wedges of red onion. Discard any remaining marinade.

★ Arrange the skewers on the barbecue and cook, with the lid closed, for 8 to 10 minutes, turning them over once, halfway through cooking time.

★ Rest 2 skewers on each flatbread, easing the meat off of the skewers, and serve with a crisp salad.

# Baked Sweet and Sour Chicken Thighs

Spiking a sweet and sour sauce with bourbon is a quick, hassle-free way of creating a delicious supper dish. Bake the chicken thighs in a wide, shallow dish (giving each thigh a little space will ensure the skins crisp up perfectly). If you have time, allow the cooked thighs to rest before you serve them. You'll lose a little of the warmth, but it will allow the flavors to develop beautifully.

**SERVES 4**

1¼ cups sweet and sour sauce

⅓ cup Jim Beam® Bourbon

8 chicken thighs (about 2½ lb.), on the bone and skin on

2 tablespoons canola oil

1¼ cups white or brown rice

¾ cup frozen peas

salt and pepper

★ Preheat the oven to 400°F.

★ Pour the sweet and sour sauce into a large baking pan and stir in the bourbon.

★ Rub the chicken thighs with the oil and season with salt and pepper. Arrange the thighs in the pan on top of the sauce and bake for 45 minutes.

★ Once the cooking time has elapsed, remove the pan from the oven and let the meat rest, uncovered, for 5 to 10 minutes while you cook the rice.

★ Cook the rice following the package directions and, during the final 2 minutes of cooking, add the frozen peas.

★ Serve the chicken on a bed of rice in warmed bowls, drizzled with any sauce remaining in the baking pan.

# Roast Chicken with Jim's Gravy

Once you try this method for cooking a chicken, you'll never go back. Bourbon is added to the dish while the meat roasts, steaming the flavor deeply into the meat and making the most incredible gravy that's rich, dark, delicious, and perfect for pouring.

**SERVES 4**

1 small carrot, coarsely cut into chunks

2 celery stalks, coarsely cut into chunks

1 red onion, coarsely cut into wedges

2 garlic cloves, unpeeled

1 whole chicken (about 3¾ lb.)

1 teaspoon canola oil

½ cup Jim Beam® Bourbon

3 tablespoons water

1 teaspoon soy sauce

⅔ cup fresh chicken stock or water

salt and pepper

★ Preheat the oven to 425°F.

★ Put the carrot, celery, onion, and garlic into a medium roasting pan and place the chicken on top. Cover the chicken skin with the oil and season with salt and pepper. Roast for 20 minutes.

★ Remove the pan from the oven and reduce the oven temperature to 400°F. Pour the bourbon and measured water into the roasting pan, then return the pan to the oven and cook for another hour, or until the juices run clear when the chicken is pierced with a knife. Remove the pan from the oven.

★ Lift up the chicken and tip the juices from the cavity all over the vegetables in the roasting pan. Transfer the chicken to a plate, cover loosely with aluminum foil, and set aside to rest while you make the gravy.

★ Place the roasting pan over low heat on the stove and mash in the garlic cloves, discarding their paper skins. Stir in the soy sauce and chicken stock or water and simmer gently for 5 minutes. Strain the gravy into a gravy boat, pressing the vegetables against the sieve to squeeze out as much of their juice as possible. Serve the chicken with the gravy along with your favorite accompaniments.

# Duck Breast with Roasted Sesame Noodles

Duck breast pairs beautifully with bourbon-roasted vegetables in this tasty dinner dish. It's deceptively easy, too, since the noodles and vegetables are cooked together in a zingy, Asian-inspired sauce. Roasting the noodles brings out a range of textures, and they absorb the flavor of everything they're cooked with. If you've never tried roasting noodles before, give this recipe a try.

**SERVES 4**

4 large duck breasts (skin on)

1 lb. 5 oz. precooked or "straight to wok" medium egg noodles

1 red bell pepper, sliced

3 fat scallions, trimmed and halved lengthwise

salt and pepper

For the dressing

juice of 2 limes

3 tablespoons soy sauce

3 tablespoons liquid honey

2 teaspoons sesame oil

2 tablespoons canola oil

1 tablespoon sesame seeds

3 tablespoons Jim Beam® Bourbon

★ Season the duck breasts well with salt and pepper, then place them, skin-side down, in a nonstick skillet set over medium heat. Cook for 6 to 8 minutes, until the skin has a good color and is crisp. As they cook, carefully spoon off the rendered fat and reserve it. Turn the duck breasts over in the pan, turn off the heat, and let rest.

★ Preheat the oven and a large nonstick baking pan to 400°F.

★ To make the dressing, combine the lime juice, soy sauce, honey, and sesame oil in a small bowl or sauce boat, then divide the mixture into 2 equal portions. Whisk the canola oil and sesame seeds into one portion and set aside. Whisk the bourbon and 2 tablespoons reserved rendered duck fat into the remaining portion.

★ Put the noodles, red bell pepper, and scallions into a large bowl, drizzle with the bourbon-laced dressing, and toss thoroughly to combine. Tip the noodle mixture onto the hot pan and roast for 10 minutes. Now place the duck breasts on the top of the noodles along with any juices from resting, and roast in the oven for another 15 minutes.

★ Slice the duck and serve on a bed of noodles, drizzled with the sesame seed dressing.

# Bourbon-Glazed Salmon Fillets

Just a few ingredients thrown into a pan are all it takes to make an awesome glaze for these salmon fillets, and it can even be made in advance if you're pushed for time. For an added twist, you can swap the Jim Beam® Bourbon for Jim Beam® Honey. Simply substitute the same amount, but reduce the quantity of brown sugar to taste.

**SERVES 4**

1 teaspoon fennel seeds

2 garlic cloves

pinch of sea salt flakes

¼ cup Jim Beam® Bourbon, plus extra to loosen

finely grated zest and juice of 1 lemon

2 tablespoons soy sauce

2 heaping tablespoons soft brown sugar

1 tablespoon canola oil

4 salmon fillets (skin on)

★ Preheat the oven to 400°F.

★ Using a mortar and pestle, crush the fennel seeds, then add the garlic and salt and crush together.

★ Pour the bourbon into a small saucepan, bring to a boil, and simmer for 2 minutes. Add the fennel and garlic mixture, lemon zest and juice, soy sauce, and sugar and let simmer for another 4 to 5 minutes. Once the surface of the glaze is covered in bubbles, set it aside to cool slightly and thicken. Add a splash of bourbon to loosen the mixture a little.

★ Put the salmon fillets on a baking pan, rub the flesh with the oil, then roast for 8 to 10 minutes, until pale all over and nearly cooked. Meanwhile, preheat the broiler on a medium setting.

★ Once the roasting time has elapsed, remove the salmon from the oven and pat dry with paper towels. Brush the glaze onto each fillet and drizzle with any that remains. Broil for 4 minutes, until the glaze caramelizes and the salmon is cooked through. Serve drizzled with the melted glaze from the baking pan.

# Pan-Fried Fish with Burnt Whiskey Butter

Perfect for a stylish dinner party, this recipe blends bourbon with pink peppercorns to make a sophisticated burnt butter sauce. It works well with just about any white fish, but try to find something thick and meaty for a sumptuous, luxurious meal. Avoid moving the fish around in the pan too much during cooking, to keep it in one piece.

---

**SERVES 4**

For the potatoes

**1½ lb. round red or round white potatoes**

**2 tablespoons unsalted butter**

**handful of chives, finely snipped**

**pinch of salt**

For the burnt whiskey butter

**2 teaspoons pink peppercorns**

**3 tablespoons Jim Beam® Bourbon**

**zest and juice of 1 lemon**

**6 tablespoons unsalted butter**

**salt**

For the fish

**2 heaping tablespoons all-purpose flour**

**1¼ lb. white fish fillets, cut into 4 pieces**

**1 tablespoon canola oil**

**salt and pepper**

★ Put the potatoes into a saucepan of water, bring to a boil, and boil for 15 to 20 minutes, or until tender.

★ Meanwhile, prepare the burnt whiskey butter and the fish. To make the butter, crush the pink peppercorns using a mortar and pestle, then mix in the bourbon, lemon zest, and half the lemon juice. Set aside.

★ Now prepare the fish. Put the flour onto a plate and season generously with salt and pepper. Pat the fish dry with paper towels, place them in the seasoned flour, and roll them over to coat. Then shake off any excess flour.

★ Heat a large nonstick skillet over medium-high heat. Add the oil, then fry the fish for 2 to 3 minutes on each side until nearly cooked through. Carefully remove the fish pieces from the pan, loosely enclose them in aluminum foil, and set aside to rest.

★ Use the pan in which you cooked the fish to finish making the whiskey butter. Wipe the hot pan carefully with paper towels and place it back over medium-low heat. Add the butter. It will instantly melt and foam and, soon afterward, turn brown and become still. At this point, stand back and add the bourbon, peppercorn, and lemon mixture (it will spatter) and let it bubble for 2 to 3 minutes, then remove the pan from the heat, taste, and season with more lemon juice or salt, as necessary.

★ While the whiskey butter mixture is cooking, drain and halve the boiled potatoes, and return them to the pan. Add the butter, chives, and salt and toss to coat the potatoes.

★ Serve the fish drizzled with burnt whiskey butter, with the potatoes alongside.

# Harvest Chili with Mixed Beans

A big, hearty chili is hard to beat, and this vegetarian version is a sure-fire winner.
You can use cans of mixed beans, or mix and match any combination of lima beans, chickpeas,
cannellini beans, kidney beans, navy beans, or pinto beans. Try to cut all of your vegetables
to roughly the same size to help everything cook evenly. (Shown on pages 94–95.)

**SERVES 4**

For the chili

2 tablespoons olive oil

1 large onion, finely chopped

2 garlic cloves, minced or crushed

1½ teaspoons ground cumin

1 teaspoon sweet smoked paprika
(optional)

½ to 1 teaspoon chili powder

heaping ½ teaspoon ground
cinnamon

½ cup Jim Beam® Bourbon

2 red, orange, or yellow bell peppers,
chopped

1 zucchini, chopped

1 sweet potato, peeled and chopped

2 x 14-oz. cans mixed beans, drained

24-oz. jar passata or can tomato
puree

1 heaping teaspoon soft dark brown
sugar

salt and pepper

large handful of fresh cilantro,
leaves coarsely chopped, to garnish

To serve

plain boiled rice (white or brown)

sour cream

grated sharp cheddar cheese

1 lime, cut into wedges

★ Heat the olive oil in a large Dutch oven or heavy saucepan over medium heat. Add the onion and fry for 7 to 8 minutes, until softened and golden. Stir in the garlic and fry for another 2 minutes. Now stir in the ground spices and fry for 1 minute. Pour in the bourbon and let simmer for 1 minute.

★ Tip in all the vegetables, the drained beans, and the passata or tomato puree. Add water to the passata jar or tomato puree can until it is about half full, then add it to the pan. Stir in the sugar and season with salt and pepper. Simmer, partially covered, over medium-low heat for 30 minutes, stirring from time to time and adding more water if needed to stop the mixture from drying out.

★ Taste the mixture to check the seasoning, then sprinkle with the fresh cilantro. Serve with rice on the side and with bowls of sour cream, grated cheese, and lime wedges.

# Macaroni and Cheese with Bourbon Crust

Here's a warm, home-style dish, spiked with bourbon-infused bread crumbs for an added crunchy kick. What's not to love? If you're making this ahead of time, don't mix the macaroni into the cheese sauce until you're almost ready to serve, to prevent it from becoming soggy.

**SERVES 4**

2 cups dry elbow macaroni

2¼ cups milk

3 tablespoons unsalted butter

2 tablespoons all-purpose flour

1 teaspoon mustard powder

¾ cup grated cheddar cheese

generous pinch of salt

For the topping

1¼ cups ciabatta bread crumbs

½ cup grated Parmesan cheese

1 tablespoon thyme leaves

3 tablespoons Jim Beam® Bourbon

2 tablespoons olive oil

salt

★ Bring a large pan of salted water to a boil over high heat. Add the macaroni and cook following the package directions. Drain the macaroni, rinse it thoroughly, then set aside in the colander to drain further.

★ Preheat the broiler and an ovenproof dish measuring approximately 8 x 12 inches on the highest setting.

★ Warm the milk until warm (not hot) in a small saucepan set over low heat, ensuring it does not boil.

★ Melt the butter in a large saucepan set over medium heat. When it is frothy, add the flour and mustard powder, mix well, and cook for 1 minute. Add the warm milk, whisking continuously, and continue to whisk while the mixture cooks for another 3 to 5 minutes, until it thickens slightly. Reduce the heat to the lowest setting and whisk in the cheese until the sauce is smooth. Season with the salt.

★ Add the drained macaroni to the cheese sauce and increase the heat a little. Stir thoroughly to combine and warm through, but do not let it come to a boil.

★ Meanwhile, stir the topping ingredients together thoroughly to combine.

★ Transfer the pasta and cheese sauce into the warmed ovenproof dish and spread the topping evenly over the surface. Broil for 4 to 6 minutes, or until the topping is golden and crunchy. Serve immediately.

# Bourbon-Roasted Vegetables and Cheese

This is a versatile meat-free main course for four that also works as a side dish with a difference for a group of six. It can be made in advance and cooled, to serve as a winter salad. And it reheats beautifully, too. Simply warm it slowly in a large, lidded pan with a good splash of water, and add the dressing once it has warmed up.

**SERVES 4**

1 cup small green/brown or
   Puy lentils

5¾ oz. soft goat cheese or feta

pepper

For the dressing

⅓ cup Jim Beam® Bourbon

3 tablespoons liquid honey

3 tablespoons soy sauce

finely grated zest and juice of
   1 large lemon

½ to 1 teaspoon chili powder

½ cup canola oil

For the roasted vegetables

2 carrots, thickly sliced

3 bell peppers of varying colors, cut
   into chunks

2 red onions, cut into thick wedges

3 cups quartered mushrooms

2 zucchini, cut into thick slices

1 eggplant, cut into chunks

4 fat garlic cloves, unpeeled

★ Place 2 large nonstick baking pans into the oven and preheat it to 350°F.

★ To make the dressing, put the bourbon, honey, soy sauce, lemon juice, and chili powder into a small saucepan and simmer over medium-low heat for 3 minutes. Take the pan off the heat, thoroughly whisk in the oil, and set aside.

★ Mix the carrots, bell peppers, onions, mushroom, zucchini, eggplant, and garlic in a large bowl and coat with half of the dressing from the pan. Mix the lemon zest into the remaining dressing and set aside.

★ Tip the vegetables onto the preheated pans, arrange them to ensure they sit in a single layer on each pan, and roast for 40 minutes, until cooked through.

★ Meanwhile, cook the lentils following the package directions.

★ When the vegetables are roasted, squeeze the pulp from the 4 roasted garlic cloves out of the skins into the reserved dressing and whisk thoroughly to combine. Add the dressing and lentils to the vegetables and mix well. Divide the mixture among 4 plates and crumble the cheese on top of each serving. Grind plenty of pepper onto the vegetables to serve.

# SIDE DISHES

# SIDE DISHES

# Roasted Butternut Squash

Squash comes into season during the months of fall, and this bourbon-spiked glaze works wonderfully with its natural sweetness to create a warming side dish. It's great with chicken, but also makes a perfect centerpiece for a vegetarian platter.

### SERVES 4

1 large or 2 small butternut squash
8 garlic cloves, unpeeled
4 sprigs of rosemary

For the glaze
⅓ cup Jim Beam® Bourbon
2 tablespoons olive oil
1 tablespoon liquid honey
1 teaspoon dried red chili flakes
2 tablespoons butter
sea salt flakes and pepper

★ Preheat the oven to 350°F.

★ Cut the squash lengthwise into eight (if large) or quarters (if small). Remove and discard the seeds. Place the pieces of squash, skin-side down, in a large roasting pan. Sprinkle the garlic and rosemary in among the squash.

★ To make the glaze, mix together the bourbon, olive oil, honey, and chili flakes with some sea salt and pepper in a small bowl. Drizzle this mixture over the squash, then dot with the butter. Roast for 30 minutes. Turn the squash over, drizzle with the juices using a spoon, and roast for another 15 to 30 minutes, or until the squash is tinged with brown at the edges and softened all the way through. Serve immediately.

# Charred Corn on the Cob with Whiskey Butter

Here, the trusty corn on the cob is given a supercharged bourbon butter drizzle—a perfect unexpected twist for a barbecue side dish. Simply char the corn on the barbecue or in a ridged grill pan, then drench it in the rich sauce. Make sure you have plenty of napkins at the ready!

**SERVES 4**

4 ears of corn, husks removed
splash of canola oil

For the whiskey butter
⅓ cup Jim Beam® Bourbon
½ teaspoon chili powder
2 teaspoons soy sauce
6 tablespoons unsalted butter

★ Prepare a barbecue to cook over medium-high heat, or set a ridged grill pan on the stove over medium-high heat.

★ Coat the ears of corn with the oil and place them on the barbecue or in the grill pan (or cook them in an open flame) until done to your liking, turning them over regularly.

★ To make the whiskey butter, put the bourbon into a small saucepan set over medium heat and let simmer for 3 minutes. Reduce the heat to low, add the chili powder and soy sauce, and stir to blend into the melted butter.

★ When the corn is done, transfer them to a serving plate and drizzle with most of the bourbon butter. Reserve the remainder to serve alongside the corn.

# Baked Sweet Potatoes

Sweet potatoes are the ultimate no-fuss food. Just sling them into the oven and let them do their thing. A spicy bourbon butter is a fantastic addition and takes no time at all to put together. Enjoy these as part of a picnic or barbecue. They're even great on their own for a simple weeknight dinner.

**SERVES 4**

**4 sweet potatoes, skins pierced with a fork**

For the bourbon butter

**½ cup Jim Beam® Bourbon**

**6 tablespoons salted butter**

**1 heaping tablespoon finely chopped fresh tarragon leaves**

**2 small hot red chilies, seeded and finely sliced**

**¾ cup finely grated Parmesan cheese**

**pepper**

★ Preheat the oven to 350°F.

★ Place the sweet potatoes on a baking pan and bake for 45 to 60 minutes, until cooked through.

★ To make the bourbon butter, put the bourbon into a small saucepan over high heat and let boil for 2 minutes. Meanwhile, put the butter into a shallow bowl. Once the whiskey has boiled for 2 minutes, pour it onto the butter in the bowl and mash together with a fork. Stir in the remaining ingredients and set aside. (If you are making the bourbon butter in advance, roll it into a sausage shape using plastic wrap, seal it in the plastic wrap, and refrigerate until needed.)

★ Slice open the potatoes and fill each with a dollop of butter (or a slice of the butter, if made in advance and refrigerated).

# Potato Wedges with Bourbon Barbecue Dip

Potato wedges make a great side dish to just about anything, and this intense barbecue dip, which takes less than ten minutes to prepare, helps make them extra special. The dip is mouthwateringly good with normal fries as well, or with the chicken nuggets on page 40.

**SERVES 4**

For the bourbon barbecue dip

**1 teaspoon smoked paprika**

**½ teaspoon garlic powder**

**2 tablespoons warm water**

**3 tablespoons Jim Beam® Bourbon**

**2 tablespoons soy sauce**

**⅓ cup ketchup**

**1 teaspoon molasses**

For the potato wedges

**1¾ lb. russet potatoes, cut into wedges**

**2 tablespoons canola oil**

**pinch of sea salt flakes**

★ Preheat the oven and a large nonstick baking pan to 400°F.

★ To make the potato wedges, set a steamer basket over a pan of boiling water and steam the potato pieces for 5 minutes. Tip them onto a plate lined with paper towels and set aside for a couple of minutes to let the steam evaporate, then pat dry. Transfer to a bowl, add the oil, and toss to coat. Now arrange the potato wedges on the preheated baking pan and bake for 30 minutes, until crispy on the outside and soft in the middle.

★ While the potatoes are baking, make the dip. Place the smoked paprika and garlic powder in a small bowl and add the measured warm water, and stir to combine. Set aside. Heat the bourbon in a small saucepan over medium-low heat and simmer for 2 minutes, then stir in the soy sauce, ketchup, molasses, and the water, garlic, and paprika mixture. Simmer for 5 minutes, stirring regularly, until the mixture has thickened and darkened. Transfer to a bowl and set aside to cool.

★ Sprinkle the potato wedges with salt flakes and serve with the dip.

# Bourbon Boston Beans

Boston beans are the ultimate comfort food, but we've given them a Kentucky twist by adding a good splash of bourbon into the mixture. The liquor adds a depth of flavor without overpowering the dish.

**SERVES 4**

1 tablespoon canola oil

1 white onion, finely chopped

3 garlic cloves, crushed

5½ oz. pancetta or smoked bacon, chopped

2 cloves

pinch of sea salt

1 tablespoon tomato paste

2 x 14-oz. cans navy beans, drained and rinsed

1 tablespoon Dijon mustard

1 teaspoon molasses

3 tablespoons Jim Beam® Bourbon

⅔ cup chicken stock

★ Heat a large Dutch oven over high heat, then pour in the oil. Once the oil is hot, add the onion, garlic, bacon, cloves, and salt and cook for 5 minutes, uncovered, until softened. Stir in the tomato paste and cook for 1 minute, then tip in the beans.

★ In a small pitcher or bowl, stir together the mustard, molasses, bourbon, and stock to combine, then add this to the beans in the saucepan. Stir well, then bring the mixture to a simmer. Cover the saucepan with the lid, reduce the heat to low, and cook for 30 to 40 minutes. Fish out and discard the cloves, and serve immediately.

# Bourbon Cornbread with Chili Flakes

Spike a classic cornbread by making a hot mash with Jim Beam® Bourbon, with dried red chili flakes adding an extra kick. You'll need to start this dish a little while in advance to give the mash time to absorb. This cornbread makes a fantastic side dish for the Spiked Chili Con Carne on page 70 or the Harvest Chili on page 92.

**SERVES 4**

½ cup Jim Beam® Bourbon

1 cup coarse yellow cornmeal (polenta)

½ cup buttermilk

¾ cup all-purpose flour sifted with ¾ teaspoon baking powder

pinch of salt

½ teaspoon baking soda

½ tablespoon dried red chili flakes

1 large egg

½ tablespoon liquid honey

¼ cup (½ stick) unsalted butter

★ Pour the bourbon into a small saucepan over high heat and bring to a boil. Meanwhile, put the polenta into a heatproof bowl. As soon as the bourbon comes to a boil, add it to the polenta in the bowl and stir in the buttermilk to combine. Set aside at room temperature for 3 to 6 hours.

★ Preheat the oven to 425°F.

★ Mix the flour and baking powder mixture, salt, baking soda, and chili flakes together in a bowl and set aside.

★ Whisk the egg and honey into the soaked polenta, using a balloon whisk, then add the dry ingredients and stir to combine.

★ Place the butter in an 8-inch nonstick ovenproof skillet set over high heat. When the melted butter is very hot, take out 2 tablespoons and stir this into the batter. Pour the remainder into a small bowl and set aside.

★ Place the buttery skillet back over high heat, pour the batter into the pan, and transfer the skillet to the oven. Cook for 15 minutes, until golden and firm in the middle. Remove the skillet from the oven, drizzle the cornbread with the remaining butter, and serve immediately.

# Everyday Bourbon Glaze

This spicy-sweet glaze offers a quick and easy way to bring a powerful hit of flavor to many a meal. It works superbly with lamb chops, pork chops, duck, chicken (with skin on—if you want to cook skinless poultry, try the bourbon and soy marinade on the opposite page), salmon, white fish, and vegetables. All you need to do is cook the food in the oven, on the stove, or on a barbecue as you normally would and, a few minutes before the end of the cooking time, remove it from the heat source, spread the glaze over it, then finish cooking as normal. Thick, sticky, and lightly spiced, it'll transform a plain meal into something really special.

**SERVES 4+**

2 tablespoons Jim Beam® Honey or
  Jim Beam® Bourbon
½ cup apricot jam
1½ tablespoons liquid honey
½ tablespoon canola oil
1 teaspoon dried red chili flakes
juice of ½ lime

★ Combine the ingredients in a small bowl and mix well. This glaze will keep in a sealed container in the refrigerator for up to 2 weeks.

★ Once your meat, fish, or vegetables are near to the end of cooking, brush them with some of the glaze, and continue to cook for 5 to 10 minutes.

# Simple Bourbon Marinade

Bourbon is a fantastic partner for soy sauce, and the combination makes a delicious quick-fix marinade that works with all sorts of meats and vegetables. Try it with red meat, skinless poultry, oily fish such as salmon, and hardy vegetables such as broccoli or portobello mushrooms. Best of all, there's no need to worry about marinating overnight, since the strong flavors need only 30 minutes to a couple of hours to work their magic.

**SERVES 4**

½ cup Jim Beam® Bourbon

2 shallots, minced

2 tablespoons soy sauce

1½ tablespoons balsamic vinegar

½ tablespoon canola oil

★ Put the bourbon and shallots into a small saucepan set over medium-high heat, bring to a boil, and simmer for 3 minutes, until the shallots have softened. Remove the pan from the heat and stir in the remaining ingredients until well blended. Let cool completely. This marinade will keep in a sealed container in the refrigerator for up to 3 days.

★ Pat your meat or vegetables dry. Place them in a nonmetallic bowl and mix with the marinade until well coated. Cover the bowl with plastic wrap and refrigerate for a minimum of 30 minutes, stirring the ingredients in the marinade occasionally. If you prefer, you can combine the ingredients with the marinade in a resealable plastic food bag. Simply ensure you squeeze out as much air as possible from the bag and seal it well before leaving it in the refrigerator to marinate. Discard the marinade when ready to cook.

# DESSERTS

# DESSERTS

# Bourbon Cherry Brownies

Everyone loves soft, gooey brownies, but in this recipe, we've made things even better by throwing bourbon-infused sour cherries into the mix. For an added whiskey kick, the brownies are drizzled with cherry-infused liquor once cooked to create the ultimate sticky chocolate treat.

**MAKES 16**

½ cup Jim Beam® Bourbon

¾ cup dried sour cherries

¾ cup (1½ sticks) unsalted butter, cut into 4 pieces

5½ oz. dark chocolate (minimum 70 percent cocoa solids), coarsely broken up

2 large eggs

1 cup superfine sugar

¾ cup all-purpose flour sifted with ¾ teaspoon baking powder

2 tablespoons unsweetened cocoa powder

pinch of salt

★ Put the bourbon and dried cherries into a small saucepan, bring to a boil, and let simmer for 3 minutes. Remove the pan from the heat, cover with a lid, and set aside until needed, to allow the cherries to absorb the bourbon.

★ Place the butter and chocolate pieces in a heatproof bowl set over a pan of gently simmering water and melt them together, stirring from time to time. Pour the mixture into a large mixing bowl and let cool a little.

★ Preheat the oven to 350°F. Line an 8-inch square baking pan with nonstick parchment paper.

★ Put the eggs and sugar into a mixing bowl and beat with a handheld electric mixer for 3 to 5 minutes or until smooth, glossy, and almost meringue-like. Add this to the cooled chocolate and butter mixture and continue to beat until well combined. Fold in the flour and baking powder mixture, the cocoa powder, and salt.

★ Drain the cherries, reserving the liquor. Fold the cherries into the batter.

★ Pour the batter into the prepared pan, pushing it well into the corners. Level off the top evenly using a rubber spatula or the back of a spoon.

★ Bake for 25 to 30 minutes, until the surface begins to crack but there is still a wobble in the center. When baked, pierce the surface with a skewer and drizzle with the reserved liquor (this will dampen the top, but it will soak in and make the brownies even better for it). For optimum flavor, set aside for a few hours so the brownies can absorb the liquor, and then cut into squares before serving.

# Jim Beam® Pecan Pie

Give the classic pecan pie an extra zing with a little bourbon and maple syrup. The amount of filling here is just right for a 9-inch pie plate. Be brave and fill it right to the top. Set the pie plate on a cookie sheet on a rack pulled partway out of the oven to save transferring the filled pie from your work top.

**SERVES 8 TO 10**

ready-made refrigerated single pie crust for a 9-inch pan

1½ cups pecan halves

vanilla ice cream, to serve

For the filling

½ cup (1 stick) unsalted butter

1 cup packed soft light brown sugar

¾ cup maple syrup

½ teaspoon vanilla extract

½ cup heavy cream

small pinch of salt

2 tablespoons cornstarch

3 tablespoons Jim Beam® Bourbon, divided

2 large eggs, plus 1 large egg yolk

★ Use a 9-inch pie pan that is at least 1¼ inches deep. Unroll the pie crust and press it gently into the pan and trim to fit. Prick the bottom several times with a fork, then refrigerate for 30 minutes.

★ Preheat the oven to 400°F. Line the pie crust with a sheet of nonstick parchment paper and fill with baking beans or lentils. Bake for 15 minutes, then remove the parchment paper and beans or lentils and bake for another 5 minutes, until golden. Set aside to cool.

★ Spread the pecan halves on a baking pan and place them in the oven for 5 minutes until lightly toasted. Remove from the oven and let cool. Reduce the oven temperature to 375°F.

★ To make the filling, melt the butter in a heavy saucepan over low heat. Remove the pan from the heat and gently whisk in the sugar, maple syrup, vanilla, heavy cream, and salt. Return the pan to the heat and stir for 2 to 3 minutes, until the sugar has dissolved.

★ In a small cup, mix the cornstarch with about 1 tablespoon of the bourbon to form a smooth paste. Take the saucepan off the heat and whisk in the cornstarch paste. Return the pan to the heat and whisk gently for 5 minutes, until the mixture has thickened slightly, to the consistency of heavy cream, and is smooth and glossy. Set aside to cool for 15 minutes, then whisk in the eggs, one at a time, followed by the egg yolk. Stir in the remaining bourbon and transfer the filling to a pitcher or large sauce boat.

★ Set the chilled pie pan on a cookie sheet and sprinkle the pecans into the crust. Pull the center rack partway out of the oven and place the sheet and pie onto it. Carefully pour the filling into the pie crust so it is level with the top. Bake for 35 to 40 minutes, until just set. Remove from the oven, transfer to a wire rack, and let cool completely. Serve with a scoop of vanilla ice cream.

DESSERTS

# Kentucky Carrot Cake

Here's a recipe for a decadent fruity carrot cake, with bourbon in both the batter and the frosting. You have to use full-fat cream cheese here because lowfat won't hold its shape. This delicious cake will be eaten in no time, but if you do have any leftovers, keep them refrigerated so the frosting stays fresh. The frosting quantity here gives enough to fill and top the cake. If you want to cover the sides as well, increase the quantities by half again.

**SERVES 8 TO 10**

For the cake

½ cup Jim Beam® Bourbon

¾ cup (not packed) golden raisins

1¾ cups all-purpose flour

2¾ teaspoons baking powder

1 teaspoon ground cinnamon

small pinch of salt

1 cup packed dark brown sugar

2¼ cups coarsely grated carrots

½ cup coarsely chopped pecans

finely grated zest of 1 large orange, divided

⅔ cup sunflower oil

3 eggs, lightly beaten

For the frosting

½ cup (1 stick) unsalted butter, softened

1½ cups confectioners' sugar

3 tablespoons Jim Beam® Bourbon

7 oz. full-fat cream cheese

reserved orange zest (see instructions)

2 tablespoons pecans, chopped, to decorate

★ To make the cake, pour the bourbon into a small saucepan and add the golden raisins. Heat gently, without allowing the liquid to come to a boil, for 5 minutes. Set aside to cool.

★ Preheat the oven to 400°F. Line the bottoms of two 8-inch round cake pans with nonstick parchment paper.

★ Sift together the flour, baking powder, and cinnamon into a large bowl. Mix in the salt, sugar, carrots, and nuts, and approximately two-thirds of the orange zest (reserve the rest for the frosting). Add the oil, eggs, and soaked golden raisins, along with any bourbon left in the pan, and mix thoroughly.

★ Divide the batter equally between the prepared cake pans and gently level off the tops. Bake for 25 to 30 minutes, until risen and a skewer inserted in the center of each cake comes out clean. Transfer to a rack to cool in the pans for 5 minutes, then invert the cakes onto the rack to cool completely.

★ For the frosting, put the butter and confectioners' sugar into a mixing bowl and use a handheld electric mixer to beat them together until smooth. Now gradually beat in the bourbon. Add the cream cheese and reserved orange zest and whisk until smooth.

★ When the cakes are completely cold, place one cake layer on a cake board or serving plate and top with half the frosting. Level the frosting using a metal spatula, covering the entire top surface of the cake. Align the second cake on top, then scrape the remaining frosting onto it, smoothing it out to an even thickness. Sprinkle the frosting with the chopped pecans to finish.

DESSERTS

# Fruitcake Loaf

This easy fruitcake loaf makes a satisfying mid-morning treat, but you will need to soak
the raisins in Jim Beam® Honey (or use Jim Beam® Bourbon, if you prefer) the day before you intend
to bake. This cake is best served the day after baking. It keeps getting better as time goes on!

**MAKES 12 SLICES**

1 lb. mixed dried fruit, such as vine
fruits, cherries, cranberries,
chopped mixed citrus peel,
chopped dates, chopped figs,
or chopped apricots

⅔ cup Jim Beam® Honey, divided

½ cup (1 stick) unsalted butter

½ cup (not packed) soft brown sugar

3 tablespoons apricot jam

2 small eggs

¾ cup pecans, broken into small
pieces

¾ cup all-purpose flour, sifted

½ teaspoon baking powder

★ Place the mixed fruit in a large, shallow bowl and add ½ cup of the bourbon.
Let soak for 24 hours, stirring occasionally. When preparing to bake, drain the
dried fruits and discard the liquor.

★ Preheat the oven to 350°F. Use a 9 x 5-inch loaf pan; line it with 2 layers of
nonstick parchment paper.

★ Cream together the butter, sugar, and jam, beating well until the mixture
becomes paler, then add the eggs and beat for another 3 minutes. Using
a spoon, fold in the drained fruit and the nuts.

★ In a separate bowl, sift together the flour and baking powder, then gently fold
this into the fruit and nut mixture.

★ Pour the batter into the prepared loaf pan and bake for 1 hour. Reduce the
oven temperature to 250°F. Cover the top of the loaf pan tightly with a double
layer of aluminum foil, then bake for another 30 minutes or until a skewer
inserted into the center of the loaf comes out clean.

★ Transfer to a wire rack and pierce the top of the fruitcake all over using the
skewer. Over the course of the next hour, drizzle the remaining bourbon
into the holes with a small spoon. Let the fruitcake stand to cool completely
before lifting it out of the pan by grasping the parchment paper and
transferring the loaf to a plate.

★ This fruitcake is best served the day after baking, and gets better as time
goes on. If there is any left over, it will keep for at least a week, wrapped in
aluminum foil and stored in an airtight container.

# Apple Crisp with Beam-Infused Cream

Apple partners beautifully with bourbon so, for this delicious dish, we've tripled it up by adding Jim Beam® Bourbon to the apple filling, the crisp topping, and the vanilla cream for drizzling. If you prefer, you can make this with Jim Beam® Honey instead, for a slightly sweeter taste.

**SERVES 4 TO 6**

For the topping

½ cup pecans

½ cup rolled oats

1 cup all-purpose flour

1 teaspoon ground cinnamon

small pinch of salt

½ cup (1 stick) unsalted butter, diced

½ cup light brown or turbinado sugar, plus 2 tablespoons for sprinkling

2 tablespoons Jim Beam® Bourbon or Jim Beam® Honey

For the filling

1¾ lb. apples, peeled and cored

¼ to ½ cup superfine sugar (adjust according to the sweetness of the apples)

½ cup Jim Beam® Bourbon or Jim Beam® Honey

⅓ cup maple syrup

For the bourbon cream

2 cups heavy whipping cream

3 tablespoons Jim Beam® Bourbon or Jim Beam® Honey

1 tablespoon superfine sugar

1 teaspoon vanilla extract

★ Preheat the oven to 375°F. Select a baking dish measuring approximately 8 x 12 inches and at least 1½ inches deep.

★ To make the topping, add the nuts and oats to a food processor and blitz until coarsely ground. Add the remaining topping ingredients, except the 2 tablespoons brown or turbinado sugar and the bourbon, and pulse until the mixture has the consistency of coarse bread crumbs. Set aside.

Continued on page 132 ⇒⟶

★ For the filling, chop the peeled and cored apples into coarse chunks. Tip them into a saucepan with ¼ cup of the sugar (or more, to taste) and the bourbon, cover, and cook over medium heat for 5 to 10 minutes, until the apples collapse. Stir in the maple syrup, taste, and add more sugar if needed. Spoon the mixture into the baking dish. If there is a lot of liquid, use a slotted spoon to transfer the apples, then boil the liquid for 2 to 3 minutes until it has reduced to a syrupy consistency, and add this to the baking dish.

★ Tip the topping mixture into the baking dish to cover the fruit loosely. Sprinkle the topping with the 2 tablespoons brown or turbinado sugar and the bourbon. Place the oven dish on a baking pan and transfer to the oven. Bake for 40 minutes, until the topping is golden brown and the filling is bubbling up at the edges.

★ To make the bourbon cream, lightly whip the heavy cream to very soft peaks, then whisk in the remaining ingredients.

★ Serve the crisp hot or warm with the bourbon cream on the side.

# Jim Beam® Cherry Pie

As if lacing a rich cherry pie with bourbon wasn't special enough, this dish also has a secret layer of marzipan at the bottom, and it doesn't get much better than that! To ensure a beautifully crisp crust, bake this in a metal pie pan. Serve with a scoop of vanilla ice cream. (Shown on next page.)

**SERVES 4 TO 6**

3½ cups canned black cherries, drained and halved

½ cup black cherry preserves

1½ tablespoons lemon juice

3 tablespoons Jim Beam® Bourbon

2 ready-made refrigerated rolled crusts for a 9-inch pie

7 oz. marzipan

splash of milk

½ tablespoon light brown or turbinado sugar

vanilla ice cream, to serve

★ Place the halved cherries, cherry preserves, and lemon juice in a large saucepan, and bring to a fast simmer. Let simmer, uncovered, for 20 to 25 minutes or until thick and not much liquid remains. Remove the pan from the heat, stir in the bourbon, and let cool completely.

★ Select a 9-inch pie pan. Unroll one of the crusts and gently press it into the pan (seal the other in plastic wrap, and refrigerate until needed), letting the excess dough hang over the edge. Prick the pie crust in a few places on the bottom. Roll out the marzipan to a disk about 1 inch wider than the base of the pan. Smooth this on top of the crust lining the pie pan and just up the sides. Cover the pan with plastic wrap and refrigerate for 30 minutes.

★ Preheat the oven to 400°F.

★ Once the pie crust has chilled, tip the cold cherry mixture into it, over the layer of marzipan. Brush the top edge of the crust in the pan with a little milk, then lay the remaining pie crust on top. Pinch the dough layer edges together to seal, and prick the inside edge all the way around the top with a fork to decorate. Trim off any excess dough, cutting a little away from the rim to allow for shrinkage. Brush the top with milk, cut a steam vent into the center, and sprinkle with the sugar.

★ Place the pie on a cookie sheet, transfer to the oven, and bake for 30 to 40 minutes until the crust is golden. Let cool briefly in the pan, then serve warm with a scoop of vanilla ice cream.

# Pear and Bourbon Tarte Tatin

This dessert looks impressive, but is made using a slightly easier method than a classic tarte tatin, which is traditionally cooked in one pan. If you have time, soak the pears in bourbon overnight, but in a hurry you can skip this step and it'll still taste great. Be careful when you invert the cooked tarte because some hot juices may spill out. Serve warm, with a scoop of vanilla ice cream on the side.

**SERVES 4**

3 to 4 unripe hard Bartlett pears (weighing about 14 oz.), peeled, cored, and quartered lengthwise

¼ cup Jim Beam® Honey or Jim Beam® Bourbon

2 tablespoons light brown sugar

2 tablespoons superfine sugar

2 tablespoons unsalted butter

pinch of salt

all-purpose flour, for dusting

7 oz. ready-made all-butter puff pastry dough sheet

vanilla ice cream, to serve

★ Submerge the pears in the bourbon in a shallow bowl. Cover with plastic wrap and refrigerate overnight. The next day, remove the pears, reserve the liquor, and pat the pears dry using paper towels.

★ Preheat the oven to 350°F.

★ Place both types of sugar in a small saucepan with 1 tablespoon of the reserved liquor. Set the pan over medium-high heat and let boil for 3 to 5 minutes or until the mixture becomes darker in color. Add the butter and, once melted, add the pears and salt. Cook for about 2 minutes, until the pears are warmed through and coated in the mixture. Set aside to cool.

★ Lightly dust your work surface with flour and unfold or unroll a puff pastry dough sheet onto it. Select a 9-inch pie pan and invert it over the dough sheet. Use the rim as a guide to cut out a disk, working ½ inch away from the rim. Set the dough aside while you return to the pears.

★ Arrange the pears, skin-side down, in the pie pan. Drizzle them with most of the remaining reserved liquor, reserving 2 tablespoons for serving. Cover the pears with the puff pastry and tuck the edges into the pan around the pears.

★ Place the pan on a cookie sheet and bake for 45 minutes. Let cool in the pan for 5 minutes, then place a serving plate over the top. Wearing oven mitts and holding the pan and plate tightly together, carefully and quickly flip the plate and pan over to transfer the tarte to the plate. Lift the pan off of the dish and let the tarte tatin rest for 5 minutes. To serve, drizzle ½ tablespoon of the reserved liquor over each slice, and place a scoop of vanilla ice cream on the side.

# Rhubarb and Ginger Upside-down Cake

An awesome combination of sweet buttery syrup, tart rhubarb, warm ginger, and a gentle kick of bourbon, this cake is a real treat. For added crunch, you can top it with sugar, then caramelize it with a cook's blowtorch, but it's delicious even without this. Any stone fruit, such as plums, would work well in place of rhubarb, and you can replace the Jim Beam® Bourbon with Jim Beam® Honey, if you prefer.

**SERVES 8**

**thick Greek-style full-fat plain unsweetened yogurt, to serve**

For the rhubarb syrup

**¼ cup (½ stick) unsalted butter**

**½ cup superfine sugar**

**3 tablespoons ginger syrup from a jar of preserved ginger in syrup**

**3 tablespoons Jim Beam® Bourbon**

**14 oz. rhubarb, cut into 4-inch pieces**

For the cake

**1 cup (2 sticks) unsalted butter, at room temperature**

**1 cup superfine sugar**

**3 large eggs**

**1¾ oz. preserved ginger in syrup, drained and grated**

**½ cup ground almonds**

**pinch of salt**

**1½ cups all-purpose flour sifted with 1½ teaspoons baking powder**

**1 to 3 tablespoons milk, divided**

**granulated sugar (optional)**

★ To make the rhubarb syrup, put the butter, sugar, and ginger syrup into a large saucepan and bring to a boil. Stir in the bourbon and rhubarb and, once the mixture returns to a boil, remove the pan from the heat and set aside.

★ Preheat the oven to 350°F. Take a large sheet of nonstick parchment paper, roll it into a tight ball, then flatten it out again and use it to line an 8-inch square cake pan, allowing plenty of paper to overhang the edges of the pan.

★ To make the cake, add the butter and sugar to a large bowl and beat with a handheld electric mixer for 3 minutes, until pale and fluffy. Add the eggs one at a time, beating each egg into the mixture thoroughly before adding the next. Using a large spoon, stir in the preserved ginger, ground almonds, and salt.

★ Sift in the flour and baking powder mixture. Do not beat, but stir it in just enough to combine. Add 1 tablespoon of the milk at a time, but stop adding milk when the batter begins to drop off the spoon easily.

★ Remove the rhubarb from the syrup using a slotted spoon and arrange it across the bottom of the cake pan. Pour ½ cup of the rhubarb syrup over the rhubarb in the pan, reserving the rest. Spoon the cake batter carefully over the rhubarb and syrup, easing it into the corners without disturbing the syrup.

★ Bake for 45 minutes. The cake is done when a skewer inserted in the center comes out clean. Remove the cake from the oven and, using a skewer, pierce holes into it and drizzle it with the reserved syrup. Let rest for 15 minutes.

★ Cover the pan with a large serving plate and quickly and carefully flip the plate and pan over so the cake rests on the plate. Gently peel off the parchment paper. If you like, sprinkle the rhubarb generously with the granulated sugar and caramelize it using a cook's blowtorch. Serve with Greek yogurt.

# Whiskey Baked Apples with Yogurt

As simple as a great dessert gets, this one can be thrown together at the last minute. Just put it in the oven while you're eating your main course and it'll be done by the time you're ready for it. Of course, Jim Beam® Apple is a good choice for this dish, but either Jim Beam® Bourbon or Jim Beam® Honey work well, too. Whichever style of bourbon you choose, it will give you a delicious cooking liquor to drizzle over the baked apples when you serve.

**SERVES 4**

4 apples

⅓ cup Jim Beam® Apple, divided

2¼ oz. mixed dried fruit (such as vine fruits, cherries, or cranberries)

2¼ oz. nuts (such as walnuts, pecans, or almonds), broken into small pieces

2 to 4 tablespoons light brown or turbinado sugar, to taste

2 tablespoons unsalted butter, cut into small cubes

liquid honey, to taste

3 tablespoons water

1 cup thick Greek-style full-fat unsweetened plain yogurt

★ Preheat the oven to 400°F.

★ Score the skin of each apple around the widest part. Core the apples, then place them in an ovenproof dish, ensuring they fit snugly.

★ Add the mixed fruit, nuts, and sugar to a medium bowl and stir in 3 tablespoons of the bourbon to combine.

★ Push a cube of butter into the central cavity of each apple, then fill with the fruit-and-nut mixture. Sprinkle the remaining mixture around the apples, then drizzle everything with a little honey. Cover the dish with aluminum foil.

★ Bake for 45 minutes, then remove the foil and stir in the measured water. Bake, uncovered, for another 15 minutes, until the apple flesh begins to expand underneath the skin.

★ Stir the remaining bourbon into the yogurt and sweeten the mixture with honey to taste.

★ Serve each apple with some of the syrupy sauce from the dish and the sweetened bourbon yogurt.

# New York Bourbon Cheesecake

This creamy, indulgent cheesecake keeps well in the refrigerator for a couple of days. This makes it handy for entertaining, because you can prepare it in advance and top it off with berries just before serving. If you don't have a food processor, put the graham crackers in a sturdy resealable freezer bag and bash them with a rolling pin to make the crumbs for the crust.

**SERVES 10 TO 12**

For the crust

**9 oz. chocolate-flavored graham crackers**

**½ cup (1 stick) unsalted butter, melted, plus 1 tablespoon for greasing**

**3 tablespoons light brown or turbinado sugar**

For the topping

**2½ cups full-fat cream cheese, at room temperature**

**1¼ cups superfine sugar**

**3 tablespoons Jim Beam® Bourbon**

**1 tablespoon all-purpose flour**

**1 teaspoon vanilla extract**

**pinch of salt**

**2 large eggs**

**1¾ cups sour cream, divided**

**fresh berries, to serve**

★ Preheat the oven to 400°F.

★ Select an 8-inch springform cake pan about 2¾ inches deep. Line the bottom with nonstick parchment paper. Brush the inside of the pan with melted butter.

★ To make the crust, blitz the graham crackers in a food processor until they take on the consistency of coarse crumbs. Add the melted butter and blitz again. Finally, add the light brown or turbinado sugar and blitz once to just combine. Press the mixture into the bottom of the pan, packing it in firmly. Level it off evenly using the back of a spoon, and refrigerate until needed.

★ For the topping, beat the cream cheese with a wooden spoon until it is smooth (alternatively, use a stand mixer fitted with a paddle attachment). Mix in the sugar, bourbon, flour, vanilla, and salt. Beat in the eggs one at a time, followed by ¾ cup of the sour cream. If at any point the mixture looks lumpy, use a sturdy balloon whisk instead. Pour the mixture over the chilled cheesecake crust.

★ Set the pan on a cookie sheet and transfer to the oven. Bake for 10 minutes, then reduce the oven temperature to 350°F, and bake for another 30 minutes, or until the cheesecake is partially set but still has a wobble in the middle. Turn off the oven and let the cheesecake stand in the oven with the door shut for 1 hour to set.

★ Remove the cheesecake from the oven and let cool completely at room temperature. Pour the remaining sour cream over the cheesecake and spread it to cover the surface completely. Refrigerate the cheesecake overnight. To serve, remove the cheesecake from the pan and slice. Serve chilled, topped with berries.

# Whiskey and Dark Chocolate Mousse Cake

Chocolate and bourbon—flavor combinations don't get much more appealing than that.
This rich, intense mousse cake is the perfect example. Serve it chilled, with heavy cream.
For added decadence, include Jim Beam® Double Oak Bourbon in the topping, but Jim Beam®
Bourbon will work just as well. For a slightly less potent version, omit the bourbon from
the topping, or reduce it to just 1 teaspoon. (Shown on pages 144–145.)

**SERVES 8 TO 10**

heavy cream, to serve

For the mousse cake

5½ oz. dark chocolate, broken
into pieces

¾ cup (1½ sticks) unsalted butter,
diced

¾ cup superfine sugar

2 tablespoons heavy cream

1 teaspoon vanilla extract

3 eggs

⅓ cup Jim Beam® Bourbon

For the topping

5½ oz. dark chocolate, very finely
chopped

⅔ cup heavy cream

4 teaspoons Jim Beam® Bourbon or
Jim Beam® Double Oak Bourbon

pinch of sea salt flakes, plus extra to
serve (optional)

★ Preheat the oven to 350°F. Line the bottom and insides of an 8-inch round cake
pan with nonstick parchment paper.

★ To make the mousse cake, put all the ingredients, except the eggs and
bourbon, into a large, heavy saucepan. Stir gently over low heat until the
chocolate and butter have almost melted, then remove the pan from the heat
and stir gently until the mixture is completely smooth. Let cool for 5 minutes,
then use a balloon whisk to beat in the eggs one at a time. Beat in the bourbon
until the mixture is smooth and glossy.

★ Pour the batter into the prepared pan, set it on a cookie sheet, transfer to the oven, and bake for 45 minutes, until just set but still a little soft in the middle. Let stand in the pan to cool completely.

★ For the topping, put the chocolate into a large heatproof bowl. In a saucepan, gently bring the cream to a simmer over medium heat, ensuring you do not let it come to a boil, then remove the pan from the heat and pour the hot cream over the chocolate. Let stand for 30 seconds (the heat from the cream will gradually melt the chocolate), then use a balloon whisk to mix the cream and chocolate together quickly. As soon as they come together into a smooth, shiny mixture, gradually stir in the bourbon and salt.

★ Place a serving plate over the cake pan. Holding them tightly together, quickly and carefully flip them over so the cooled cake transfers onto the plate. Carefully peel off the parchment paper (don't worry if the surface of the cake breaks up a little, because the topping will cover this). Pour the warm topping onto the cake and spread it across the top and down the sides to coat. Let cool completely, then chill in the refrigerator for at least 3 hours, or for up to 3 days.

★ Sprinkle with a little extra sea salt just before serving, if desired. Serve in thin slices with a dollop of softly whipped heavy cream.

# Bourbon Chocolate Truffles

These truffles are mind-blowing and (if you can bear to part with them) make perfect gifts. Before rolling, you can keep the mixture in the refrigerator for up to 5 days, or in the freezer for up to a month (just defrost at room temperature for about 2 hours before rolling). One word of warning: it's absolutely crucial that you don't allow the cream to boil when making the truffle mixture, or the chocolate can become grainy. For a stronger bourbon flavor, use Jim Beam® Double Oak Bourbon.

**MAKES ABOUT 30**

For the chocolate truffles

**7 oz. dark chocolate, finely chopped**

**1 cup heavy cream**

**1 tablespoon unsalted butter**

**1½ tablespoons Jim Beam® Bourbon or Jim Beam® Double Oak Bourbon**

**pinch of sea salt**

To decorate

**¼ cup unsweetened cocoa powder**

**⅔ cup finely chopped pecans, toasted**

**3½ oz. dark and/or milk chocolate, melted**

★ To make the truffles, put the chocolate into a heatproof bowl. In a saucepan, gently bring the cream and butter to a simmer over medium heat, ensuring you do not allow the mixture to come to a boil, then remove the pan from the heat and pour the mixture over the chocolate in the bowl. Let stand for 30 seconds (the heat from the cream will gradually melt the chocolate), then mix using a balloon whisk. As soon as everything has come together into a smooth, shiny mixture, gradually stir in the bourbon and mix in the salt. Set aside to cool, then cover and chill for at least 4 hours until firm (or you can freeze it at this stage).

★ To roll the truffles, remove the mixture from the refrigerator 10 minutes before starting.

★ Roll teaspoonfuls of the mixture quickly between your palms. Place the rolled truffles on a cookie sheet lined with nonstick parchment paper.

★ To decorate, put the cocoa powder into one shallow bowl, and the chopped nuts into another. Roll one-third of the truffles in cocoa powder and one-third in the chopped nuts. Coat the remaining truffles in the melted chocolate: dip them in the melted chocolate; use 2 forks to roll them in the liquid and to lift them out; then transfer them to another cookie sheet lined with nonstick parchment paper and let cool. (Once cool, you can drizzle them with a contrasting melted chocolate, if desired.) Refrigerate until ready to serve.

# Easy Chocolate, Bourbon, and Raisin Ice Cream

The beauty of this recipe is that you don't need an ice-cream maker, and you don't have to spend hours hand-churning, since the addition of Jim Beam® Bourbon keeps the ice cream silky smooth and scoopable. And the taste is absolutely incredible. Remove the ice cream from the freezer a few minutes before serving to let it soften up a little for scooping.

### SERVES 4 TO 8

For the Jim Beam® raisins

**⅔ cup Jim Beam® Bourbon**

**1 cup (not packed) raisins**

**3 tablespoons superfine sugar**

For the ice cream base

**4 egg yolks**

**¾ cup superfine sugar, divided**

**3½ oz. dark chocolate, coarsely chopped**

**1½ tablespoons unsweetened cocoa powder**

**1¾ cups heavy cream**

**½ cup milk**

**1 teaspoon vanilla extract**

**¼ teaspoon sea salt flakes**

**3 tablespoons Jim Beam® Bourbon**

★ For the Jim Beam® raisins, pour the bourbon into a small saucepan and add the raisins and sugar. Bring to a simmer, then let simmer gently over medium heat for 5 minutes. Set aside to cool. When cool, remove the raisins with a slotted spoon, then return them to any residual bourbon in the pan.

★ Put the egg yolks and ¼ cup of the superfine sugar into a large heatproof mixing bowl and, using a handheld electric mixer, beat until the mixture is thick and pale.

★ Put the chocolate and cocoa into a separate large heatproof bowl.

★ Pour the cream, milk, and remaining superfine sugar into a large heavy saucepan. Stir over medium heat until the sugar has dissolved and the mixture reaches a simmer, but don't let it come to a boil. Remove the pan from the heat and let stand for 30 seconds, then pour the mixture over the chocolate and cocoa. Whisk quickly with a balloon whisk until the chocolate has melted.

★ Very slowly add ladlefuls of the chocolate mixture to the egg yolks and sugar mixture, beating continuously with the electric mixers, until half the chocolate mixture is mixed in, after which you can pour it in more quickly. Beat in the vanilla and salt.

★ Return the mixture to the saucepan, set it over low heat, and stir it continuously for 10 minutes, or until steaming hot and thickened to the consistency of heavy cream. Pour the mixture through a sieve into a freezer-safe container, stir in the bourbon, along with the raisins and their soaking liquor, and let cool. Once cool, freeze overnight, or for up to 2 weeks, before serving.

# Kentucky Bourbon Chocolate Shake

This is the Jim Beam® take on the classic American chocolate milk shake, but feel free to adjust the recipe to suit your mood. Reduce the ice cream by ½ cup and increase the ice quantity for a thinner, less rich version, or add a splash more bourbon if you want an added kick. Place a couple of freezer-safe glasses into the freezer to chill before serving to keep things extra cool on a hot day.

**MAKES 4 SHAKES**

18 oz. (about 3½ cups) vanilla ice cream

½ cup chocolate-hazelnut spread

½ cup milk

⅓ cup Jim Beam® Honey or Jim Beam® Bourbon

1 cup ice cubes or crushed ice

★ Put all the ingredients into a blender and blend to a thick, smooth, icy consistency. Pour into glasses, add straws and a spoon, and drink right away while cold and thick.

# CLASSIC COCKTAILS

# CLASSIC COCKTAILS

# Happy Hollow Hedgerow

Nestled in the rolling foothills of Kentucky, Happy Hollow is the home of the Jim Beam American Stillhouse. This fruity summer cocktail perfectly encapsulates the feeling of the long summer evenings there. If you can't find sparkling elderflower, try using lemonade instead.

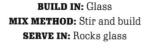

**BUILD IN:** Glass
**MIX METHOD:** Stir and build
**SERVE IN:** Rocks glass

1 part Jim Beam® Apple

1 scant part Chambord® Liqueur

3 parts sparkling elderflower, or to top off

2 to 3 fresh blackberries per drink, to garnish

★ Pour the Jim Beam® Apple and Chambord® Liqueur into a rocks glass filled with a handful of crushed ice. Stir well and top off with the sparkling elderflower. Garnish with the blackberries and serve.

# Jim's Mint Julep

A close relative of the mojito, the mint julep provides a classic way to enjoy a bourbon cocktail on a hot summer's day. It keeps things simple—just bourbon, sweetened with sugar syrup, topped off with soda water, and laced with fresh mint leaves—and is all the better for it.

**BUILD IN:** Glass
**MIX METHOD:** Stir and build
**SERVE IN:** Rocks glass

handful of mint leaves per drink

2 parts Jim Beam Black® Bourbon or
   Jim Beam® Double Oak Bourbon

½ part sugar syrup

soda water, to top off

★ Fill a rocks glass with crushed ice. Crush the mint leaves in your palm (to release the oils), then drop them into the glass. Add the bourbon and sugar syrup and stir to mix. Top off with soda water and serve.

# Apple and Maple Mule

This cocktail pairs Jim Beam® Apple with ginger ale, cut through with a dash of lime juice and balanced with the sweetness of maple syrup, to make a refreshing long drink for handing out at get-togethers. Think of this drink as a supercharged bourbon take on the classic Moscow Mule cocktail.

**BUILD IN:** Highball glass
**MIX METHOD:** Stir and build
**SERVE IN:** Highball glass

2 parts Jim Beam® Apple

½ part maple syrup

½ part freshly squeezed lime juice

8 parts ginger ale, or to top off

To garnish

slice of green apple or lime per drink

1 sprig of mint per drink

★ Pour the bourbon, maple syrup, and lime juice into a highball glass and stir well until the maple syrup has dissolved. Add a handful of ice cubes and top off with ginger ale. Garnish with a slice of apple or lime and a sprig of mint, then serve.

# Honey Beam Blush

Think of this light and fruity cocktail as a Jim Beam® take on the classic Cosmopolitan.
It's a perfect drink for a summer gathering. To really make the most of this combination,
be sure to squeeze a fresh orange rather than using juice out of a carton. It's most definitely
worth the extra effort.

**BUILD IN:** Shaker
**MIX METHOD:** Shake and strain
**SERVE IN:** Martini glass

1 part Jim Beam® Honey

2 parts cranberry juice

½ part freshly squeezed orange juice

strip of pared orange zest cut to a
width of ½ inch per drink, to
garnish

★ Pour the bourbon, cranberry juice, and orange juice into a cocktail shaker. Add 2 to 3 ice cubes and shake. Strain the mixture into a small martini glass. Twist the strip of orange zest over the glass to release the oil into the cocktail, then drop it into the drink as a garnish and serve.

# Sour Jim

A whiskey sour is a wonderful thing! And this is the ultimate recipe for one, allowing you to enjoy the unique flavors of Jim Beam®. Perfectly balanced, blending creaminess with sharp lemon juice, this drink is at its best when made with Jim Beam Black® Bourbon or Jim Beam® Double Oak Bourbon, but it's still delicious with Jim Beam® Bourbon.

**BUILD IN:** Shaker
**MIX METHOD:** Shake and strain
**SERVE IN:** Rocks glass

2 parts Jim Beam Black® Bourbon or Jim Beam® Double Oak Bourbon

1 part egg white

1 scant part freshly squeezed lemon juice

1 scant part sugar syrup

2 to 3 drops Angostura® bitters per drink, to garnish

★ Pour the bourbon, egg white, lemon juice, and sugar syrup into a cocktail shaker. Add 2 to 3 ice cubes and shake vigorously for 30 seconds. Strain the mixture into a rocks glass filled with ice cubes, garnish with Angostura® bitters, and serve.

# Clermont Champagne

A simple, light, and refreshing way to enjoy bourbon, this is the perfect
drink for serving at a special event or celebration. (Shown on page 167.)

**BUILD IN:** Glass
**MIX METHOD:** Stir and build
**SERVE IN:** Champagne flute

1 brown sugar cube per drink

2 dashes of Angostura® bitters
  per drink

1 part Jim Beam® Bourbon

4 to 5 parts sparkling wine

★ Place the sugar cube into a champagne flute. Shake the Angostura® bitters
onto the sugar cube. Pour in the bourbon and slowly top off with sparkling
wine, then serve.

# Bardstown Boulevardier

A cousin of the Negroni, this drink is named in honor of Bardstown, near the Jim Beam American Stillhouse, in the heart of Kentucky. Balancing bitter and sweet, it's a rich, warming cocktail that's best garnished with a twist of fresh orange. (Shown on page 166.)

**BUILD IN:** Glass
**MIX METHOD:** Stir and build
**SERVE IN:** Rocks glass

1 part Jim Beam® Black Bourbon or Jim Beam® Double Oak Bourbon

½ part Aperol® Aperitivo or Campari® Liqueur

½ part sweet (red) vermouth

strip of pared orange zest cut to a width of ½ inch per drink, to garnish

★ Half-fill a rocks glass with ice cubes. Add the bourbon, Aperol® Aperitivo or Campari® Liqueur, and vermouth and stir gently to combine. Garnish with a twist of orange zest and serve.

# Cherry Picker

This is a supercharged throwback to a 1950s classic—the cola float—but
with a kick. Sweet, cool, fizzy, and fun, you'll need a straw and a long spoon
to serve it up with.

**BUILD IN:** Glass
**MIX METHOD:** Stir and build
**SERVE IN:** Short-stemmed wineglass

1 to 2 scoops vanilla ice cream
  per drink

2 parts Jim Beam® Bourbon

8 to 10 parts cherry cola

1 maraschino cherry per drink, to
  garnish

★ Place a scoop of vanilla ice cream into a short-stemmed wineglass. Pour in
the bourbon, then slowly top off with cherry cola. Stir gently—it will fizz up a
little. Top with a second scoop of ice cream if you like, garnish with a cherry,
and serve with a straw and a long spoon.

# Long Lick Lemonade

Long Lick Creek runs past the Jim Beam distillery, and this homage to old-fashioned lemonade is the kind of drink that we enjoy there on lazy summer afternoons. Fizzy, zesty, and delicious, it's one to sip as you watch the sun go down.

**BUILD IN:** Glass
**MIX METHOD:** Stir and build
**SERVE IN:** Highball or rocks glass

1 part Jim Beam® Bourbon

1 part sugar syrup

½ part freshly squeezed lemon juice

thin strip of pared orange zest
  per drink

tonic or soda water, to taste

★ Fill a highball glass or rocks glass with a handful of ice cubes. Add the bourbon, sugar syrup, lemon juice, and orange zest. Stir gently to combine, top off with tonic or soda water, and serve.

# Jim Beam® Maple Fizz

Maple, with its sweet, woody flavor, goes very well with bourbon, and this fizzy cocktail makes the most of that happy marriage. Like the Sour Jim (see page 162), it's made with egg white to add creaminess, and spiked with sharp lemon juice to balance the flavors, for an intriguing and refreshing drink.

**BUILD IN:** Shaker
**MIX METHOD:** Shake and build
**SERVE IN:** Highball glass

1½ parts Jim Beam® Bourbon

scant part maple syrup

½ part freshly squeezed lemon juice

a dash of heavy cream per drink

1 part egg white

3 parts soda water, or to top off

1 whole star anise or slice of lemon
per drink, to garnish (optional)

★ Pour the bourbon, maple syrup, lemon juice, heavy cream, and egg white into a cocktail shaker. Add 2 to 3 ice cubes and shake vigorously for 30 seconds.

★ Fill a highball glass with ice cubes. Strain the mixture over the ice and top off with soda water. Garnish the cocktail with a star anise or lemon slice if you like, and serve.

# Kentucky Manhattan

Warm, smoky, and bitter, this cocktail brings to mind the classic Manhattan. It's a sophisticated drink that beautifully balances the vanilla notes of bourbon with aromatic vermouth.

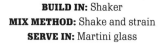

**BUILD IN:** Shaker
**MIX METHOD:** Shake and strain
**SERVE IN:** Martini glass

**2 parts Jim Beam Black® Bourbon or Jim Beam® Double Oak Bourbon**

**a dash of Jim Beam® Bourbon (optional) per drink**

**½ part sweet (red) vermouth**

**2 dashes Angostura® bitters per drink**

**1 maraschino cherry per drink, to garnish**

★ Pour the bourbon, vermouth, and bitters into a cocktail shaker. Add 2 to 3 ice cubes and shake vigorously for 30 seconds. Strain into a martini glass, garnish with a maraschino cherry, and serve.

# Old Fashioned

This smooth cocktail, with a hint of sweetness, brings out the very best in Kentucky bourbon. An Old Fashioned goes perfectly with meaty dishes such as burgers and steaks, so load up your glass with plenty of ice and enjoy it at a hot summer barbecue.

**BUILD IN:** Glass
**MIX METHOD:** Stir and build
**SERVE IN:** Rocks glass

**2 parts Jim Beam Black® Bourbon or Jim Beam® Double Oak Bourbon**

**a dash of sugar syrup per drink**

**a dash of orange bitters per drink**

**a dash of Angostura® bitters per drink**

**thin strip of pared orange zest per drink, to garnish**

★ Half-fill a rocks glass with ice cubes. Add the bourbon, then the sugar syrup and bitters, and stir for 1 minute until the ice begins to melt slightly and the ingredients are thoroughly blended.

★ Fill the glass with more ice cubes. Twist the strip of orange peel, add it to the cocktail to garnish, then serve.

# Old Fashioned Kentucky Mud

Ever wondered what an Old Fashioned crossed with a Mississippi mud pie would taste like?
Well, wonder no more! This sweet cocktail enhances the combination of Jim Beam® Bourbon and
Jim Beam® Honey by giving them a fantastic chocolate twist.

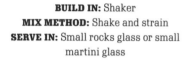

**BUILD IN:** Shaker
**MIX METHOD:** Shake and strain
**SERVE IN:** Small rocks glass or small
martini glass

1 part Jim Beam® Bourbon

1 part Jim Beam® Honey

½ part dark chocolate sauce

1 teaspoon crushed honeycomb
   (sponge toffee) or honeycomb
   chocolate bar per drink,
   to garnish (optional)

★ Pour the Jim Beam® Bourbon, Jim Beam® Honey, and chocolate sauce into a
cocktail shaker. Add 2 to 3 ice cubes and shake vigorously for 30 seconds.
Strain the cocktail into a small rocks glass or martini glass, garnish with the
honeycomb, if using, and serve.

# Berries and Cream Beam

Cocktail or dessert? The Berries and Cream Beam straddles both, blending Jim Beam® Bourbon with raspberry liqueur, cream, and a tried-and-tested partner—chocolate—with delicious results. Sweet and smooth, this tempting treat is for those who like their cocktails luxurious.

**BUILD IN:** Shaker
**MIX METHOD:** Shake and strain
**SERVE IN:** Martini glass

1½ parts Jim Beam® Bourbon

scant part Chambord® Liqueur

½ part dark chocolate sauce or dark crème de cacao

½ part heavy cream

pinch of powdered chocolate drink mix per drink, to garnish

★ Pour the bourbon, Chambord® Liqueur, chocolate sauce or crème de cacao, and cream into a cocktail shaker. Add 2 to 3 ice cubes and shake vigorously. Strain into a martini glass. Sprinkle with the powdered chocolate and serve.

# Jim's Winter Cup

Perfect for those long winter nights, this is a warming hug in a mug. If you don't have a vanilla bean you can add a small dash (about ¼ teaspoon) of vanilla extract instead. For a fun garnish, serve with a cinnamon stick stirrer.

**BUILD IN:** Saucepan
**MIX METHOD:** Heat, stir, and build
**SERVE IN:** Mug or heatproof glass

10 parts cloudy apple juice

a pinch of dark brown sugar
  per drink

1 cinnamon stick (about
  2 inches long) per drink

½ vanilla bean (split lengthwise)
  per drink

2 cloves per drink

1 whole star anise per drink
  (optional)

1½ parts Jim Beam Black® Bourbon
  or Jim Beam® Double Oak Bourbon

To garnish

1 slice of lemon per drink

1 cinnamon stick per drink
  (optional)

★ Pour the apple juice into a small saucepan with the sugar and spices. Stir over low heat for 3 to 5 minutes, ensuring the liquid does not come to a boil.

★ Remove the pan from the heat and stir in the bourbon, then strain into a mug or heatproof glass. Add a slice of lemon and a cinnamon stick to stir, if using. Serve hot.

# Tale of Two Beams

This drink can be described as an Irish coffee, Kentucky style. It's made by blending two different varieties of Jim Beam® (although, in a pinch, you can stick with one variety and increase the quantity accordingly), and mixing it with dark, bitter coffee. Be sure to use good-quality, freshly brewed strong coffee for maximum impact.

**BUILD IN:** Heatproof glass
**MIX METHOD:** Stir and build
**SERVE IN:** Heatproof glass

8 parts freshly brewed, hot filter coffee

a generous pinch of brown sugar per drink

1½ parts Jim Beam Black® Bourbon or Jim Beam® Double Oak Bourbon

2 parts heavy cream

½ part Jim Beam® Honey

★ Pour the hot coffee into a heatproof glass and stir in the sugar and the Jim Beam Black® or Jim Beam® Double Oak.

★ Whip the heavy cream with the Jim Beam® Honey in a small pitcher to very soft peaks. Be careful not to overwhip the mixture because you want a thick liquid, not whipped cream. Spoon the cream gently over the coffee, so that it floats on top, and serve.

# Index

# Notes on the Recipes

Standard level spoon measurements are used in all recipes unless otherwise specified.

The cocktail recipes in this book have been based on a part being 1 fl. oz. If preferred, a different volume can be used, providing the proportions are kept constant within a drink and suitable adjustments are made where needed.

Eggs should be medium-size unless otherwise stated. This book contains dishes made with raw or lightly cooked eggs. The U.S. Food and Drug Administration advises that certain people, including children, older adults, pregnant women, and people with weakened immune systems (such as transplant recipients and individuals with HIV/AIDS, cancer, or diabetes), should avoid consuming raw or lightly cooked eggs, and should use pasteurized eggs/egg products when preparing recipes that call for raw or undercooked eggs. Once prepared, these dishes should be kept refrigerated and used promptly.

Pepper should be freshly ground black pepper unless otherwise stated.

This book includes dishes made with nuts and nut derivatives. It is advisable for customers with known allergic reactions to nuts and nut derivatives and those who may be potentially vulnerable to these allergies, such as pregnant and nursing mothers, invalids, the elderly, babies, and children, to avoid dishes made with nuts and nut oils. It is also prudent to check the labels of prepackaged ingredients for the possible inclusion of nut derivatives.

# ABOUT
# JIM BEAM®

SEVEN GENERATIONS, more than 200 years and just one goal:
to make the best bourbon in the world.

Today, Jim Beam® is the WORLD'S NO.1 BOURBON, enjoyed throughout
the world, from our hometown in Kentucky to every corner of the globe.
But we're far from an overnight success—founded in 1795, our passion
for making truly great bourbon has been passed down from generation
to generation.

A lot has changed in the 220 or so years since Jacob Beam sold his first
barrel of "Old Jake Beam Sour Mash" whiskey, but we're proud to say
that things at Jim Beam® have remained more or less the same.
We still use the same key ingredients and the same basic process, aging
our bourbon in charred oak barrels for twice as long as the law requires
to ensure the perfect smooth flavor in every batch.

Nowadays, the Beam family has grown, and you can enjoy a range
of bourbons to suit your taste. But with all of our experience being
poured into every bottle, you know that you're enjoying
THE WORLD'S FINEST BOURBON.